FLORENCE
PISA
SIENA

SAN GIMIGNANO

BONECHI
edizioni il Turismo
FIRENZE - 1954

© Copyright 2000 by Bonechi Edizioni "Il Turismo" S.r.l.
Via dei Rustici, 5 - 50122 Florence - Italy
Phone +39-055.239.82.24/25
Fax +39-055.21.63.66
E-mail: barbara@bonechi.com
         bbonechi@dada.it
http://www.bonechi.com
Printed in Italy

The article on the Museum of the Sinopias in Pisa was written by: **Antonio Chinca**
Cover and layout: Claudia Baggiani
Photographs: Archivio della Bonechi Edizioni "Il Turismo" S.r.l.
Photographs: I-Buga S.a.s. Milano; Paolo Bacherini;
             Niccolò Orsi Battaglini
Printed by: BO.BA.DO.MA, Florence
ISBN 88-7204-274-7

FLORENCE

The origins of Florence go back to the Etruscan era when Fiesole dominated the valley from the hilltop. Groups of settlers went down to the banks of the Arno to found a village, modest, but destined to thrive thanks to its favorable position on the direct line of communication between the north and south of Italy, although it was very vulnerable to enemy attacks and invasions. The Romans soon founded a colony here with the auspicious name Florentia (that is, "destined to flourish"). By the 2nd century B.C. the new municipality was pre-eminent among the cities of the Roman Tuscia. The town survived the Dark Ages to emerge slowly in the Carolingian period, first as the fief of the marchesi of Tuscany, among whom Ugo and Matilda are worth remembering. From the 11th century on, Florence began to acquire greater autonomy. In 1115 after the struggles against the simoniacal clergy and the feudal lords of the surrounding districts,

Piazza della Signoria, during the most recent excavations, undertaken from 1982-1989 when the square was repaved.

the Commune of Florence had virtually come into being. Ten years later the new state defeated her rival, Fiesole. Soon, inside the city which was now surrounded by a new circle of walls, the first clashes began to take place between the feudal lords who had moved into the city and the artisans who had formed the powerful guilds. These clashes led to the development of two factions, the Guelphs (who supported the Pope) and the Ghibellines (who backed the Emperor), with the former clearly dominating. At the end of the 13th century the internal rivalry made the Guelphs split into two parties, the "blacks" and the "whites". The blacks, supported by the Pope, forced many of the whites, including Dante Alighieri, into exile. In the meantime, and in spite of these internal problems, Florence was becoming more powerful, fighting against rival cities (Pistoia, Arezzo, Volterra, Siena) and expanded her territory. In the cultural and economic fields, at the turn of the 13th-14th

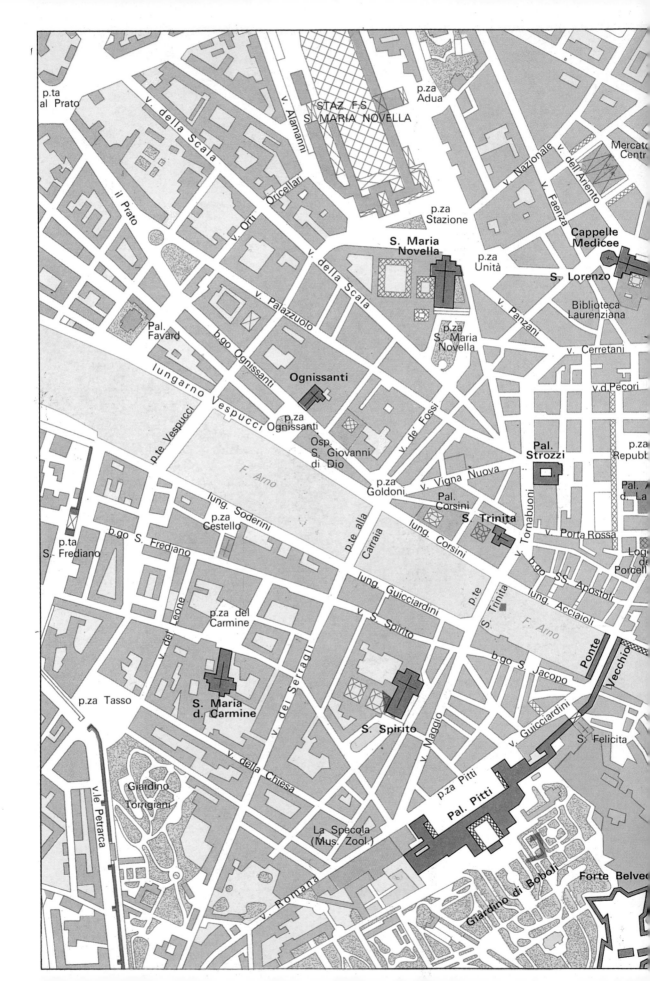

From the left: *Portrait of Bia, Natural Daughter of Cosimo I de'Medici* and *Portrait of Eleonora di Toledo with Her Son,* both by *Agnolo Bronzino* (Uffizi Gallery); below: *Coats of Arms of three of the major guilds: Silk* (left), *Wool* (centre), *Judges and Notaries* (right).

century Florence was becoming one of the most important centers in Italy. It was the era of the great banking and merchant families when the wool and silk industries flourished. The early decades of the 14th century, were marked by many political and economic vicissitudes, first the battles against the last of the Ghibellines, and then during the rules of Carlo di Calabria and Gualtieri di Brienne, Duke of Athens (1343). The terrible outbreak of the plague which Boccaccio describes in the Decameron occurred in 1348. By the end of the century, the conflicts between the "popolo grasso", that is the rich middle class that ruled the city through the Guilds and the "popolo minuto", the poor working classes were becoming more violent. The struggle came to a head in the "Tumulto dei Ciompi" (the revolt of the humble workers of the Wool Guild), through which the lower classes came to power in 1378. Soon afterwards, however, the oligarchy, headed by the Albizi family regained ascendancy, through its support of the popolo minuto. The rich Medici family was acquiring increasing political power, and soon the rule of the Signoria was established, although republican appearances were preserved. Cosimo the Elder, founder of the Medici Signoria, was succeeded by Lorenzo the Magnificent, a shrewd statesman and great patron of the arts. The century that culminated in the rule of the Magnificent (he died in 1492) was one of the most brilliant in Florentine history, especially in the field of culture and art. It was the age of Humanism and the great art of the Renaissance. Between the end of the 15th and the beginning of the 16th centuries, the city became a free Republic, after having banished Lorenzo's successor, Piero. The dominant figure in this period was Girolamo Savonarola. The Medici returned, however, and Florence remained under their rule until 1527 when yet another revolt restored the republican institutions. But the Medici, supported by both the Holy Roman Emperor and the pope, returned once more after a harsh siege (1530). Despite the political unrest, the years between the end of the 15th and early 16th centuries were rich in great personalities in the fields of art and literature (Michelangelo and Guicciardini). In 1569 Cosimo dei Medici, ruler of the city, received the title of Grand Duke which passed on to his heirs. Cosimo was succeeded by his son, Francesco I, a lover of the arts and letters

Portrait of Frà Girolamo Savonarola by *Frà Bartolomeo* (Museum of San Marco).

The Execution of Girolamo Savonarola, sixteenth century panel (Museum of San Marco).

who had little skill as a statesman. The following century marked the beginning of the city's decline. International factors (the preponderance of the great powers of France, Austria and Spain, and the northward shift of the centers of economic power) and the lack of significant personalities among the Medici Grand Dukes (with the exception of Ferdinando II), all combined to exclude Florence, like the rest of Italy from the category of European powers. When the dynasty died out with the death of Gian Gastone (1737) and the Grand Duchy passed over to the Lorraine family that was related to the ruling house of Austria, Florence regained a certain, albeit marginal, amount of importance in Europe. The Lorraines ruled the Grand Duchy continuously, except for the period of the Napoleonic domination (1799-1814), until Florence and Tuscany became part of the united Italy (1859). Florence was capital of the new Kingdom of Italy from 1865 to 1871. The city continued to be, as it is now, a lively artistic and cultural center. It was severely damaged during World War II, and again by the disastrous flood in 1966 (all of which was repaired by intensive and careful restorations).

Portrait of Cosimo the Elder, attributed to *Pontormo* (Uffizi Gallery); below and right: *two views of the parade and flag-wavers of the "calcio in costume",* the historic football game played in Renaissance costume.

FOLKLORE

There are two traditional events in Florence. In the Middle Ages, as today, the **"Calcio in Costume"**, ancestor of modern soccer consisted of a series of games played by the teams of the districts of Santa Croce, San Giovanni, Santa Maria Novella and Santo Spirito in May and June. The prize was a calf.

The other is the **Explosion of the Cart** and the tradition dates back to the First Crusade. This is a Florentine event that takes place in front of the cathedral on Easter Sunday. A huge cart, known as the "Brindellone" is set afire by a "dove" filled with firecrackers that runs along a wire stretched from the altar inside the cathedral to the square in front. The Florentines can "read" auspices for the year, and mainly for the harvests, from the dove's flight.

PIAZZA DEL DUOMO

At the dawn of the Middle Ages, the site of the Piazza Duomo was crowded with private dwellings and public buildings. The church of Santa Reparata was built over the foundations of one of the latter in the 4th century. Three centuries later (though some sources believe it was the same century) the Baptistry was erected next to the church and the place soon became the center of religious life in Florence. Santa Reparata became a cathedral in 1128, but it was soon too small for this new role and greater dignity - the population was growing too - and in 1289 the Commune decided to enlarge it. This was part of an extensive rebuilding plan that involved expanding the city's walls (the Roman circle was too small), the construction of the Prior's Palace (now Palazzo Vecchio) and alterations to existing buildings such as Santa Croce, the Badia, Orsanmichele, the Bargello and the Baptistry. In order to create a city that would be new but harmonious, one man, Arnolfo di Cambio was given the responsibility of directing and coordinating the works. One of the greatest architects and sculptors of his time, he raised the level of the piazza (which he had re-paved), eliminating the podium on which the Baptistry had stood, demolished some houses nearby and began building the new cathedral for which he planned a dome and exterior decorations matching those on the Baptistry. Arnolfo's death in 1302 put a stop to the work which was resumed in 1332-34 with the construction of the Bell Tower. Filippo Brunelleschi built the dome (1420-36) that gave the building its final appearance, although the Gothic-style façade was actually done in the 19th century.

Aerial view of Piazza del Duomo.

Opposite: *the Baptistry*; lower left: *the North Door*, by *Lorenzo Ghiberti* (1403-1424); lower right: *Vittorio Ghiberti and Lorenzo Ghiberti*, details on the famous Door of Paradise.

THE BAPTISTRY

Dante's "Bel San Giovanni", the religious building most beloved by the Florentines was perhaps started in the 7th century, but the work done in the 11th-12th centuries made it the most important monument of Romanesque architecture in Florence. For centuries its regular octagonal shape and the symmetrical arrangement of the exterior decorations were an architectural ideal for artists of the stature of Arnolfo, Giotto, Brunelleschi, Leon Battista Alberti, Leonardo and Michelangelo. It has three magnificent bronze doors. The **South Door**, by Andrea Pisano (c. 1330) consists of 28 panels illustrating *The Life of the Baptist*. The **North Door** is by Ghiberti, executed in 1403-1424. The 28 panels depict episodes from the *Life of Christ*.

THE DOOR OF PARADISE

The famous East Door, or the "Door of Paradise" as Michelangelo called it was sculpted by Lorenzo Ghiberti between 1425 and 1452 with the help of his sons Vittorio and Tommaso, Benozzo Gozzoli and Michelozzo. Of the twenty-seven years it took to complete the work, sixteen were devoted to chiseling after the casting. Ghiberti worked in full Renaissance spirit, abandoning the Gothic style of the North Door. The subjects of the ten panels are: *The Creation of Adam and Eve; Original Sin; the Expulsion from Eden; Adam and Eve at Work; the Killing of Abel; the Drunkenness of Noah; Three Angels appear to Abraham; the Sacrifice of Isaac; Jacob and Esau; Scenes from the Life of Joseph; of Moses, of Joshua; of David;* and then *Solomon and the Queen of Sheba.*

Below: *The Door of Paradise* by *Lorenzo Ghiberti*; right: *panels from the Door of Paradise* depicting *King Solomon greeting the Queen of Sheba in the Temple* (top), *The Battle Against the Philistines* (center), *Moses Receiving the Tables of the Law on Mount Sinai* (bottom).

The interior of the Baptistry; below: *Christ and the Last Judgement,* detail of the inside of the Baptistry Dome.

THE INTERIOR - The vault of the Tribune is covered with 13th century mosaics, the work of Fra' Jacopo called Scarsella after this part of the Baptistry ("pocket") that forms a rectangular projection from the rest of the structure. The monolithic columns in the walls, some of Oriental granite, others of cipollin marble, were taken from other buildings. The splendid floor is inlaid in black, white, red and green marble. Near the Door of Paradise is a large slab, placed by Strozzo Strozzi in the 11th century depicting *the Ptolemaic cosmic system with the sun and the signs of the Zodiac.* The inscription around the sun "En giro torte sol cicles et roto igne" which can also be read backwards, means "I sun, with fire, turn the circles and turn myself."

THE CUPOLA

The 13th and 14th century mosaics that cover the inside of the Baptistry cupola were done by artists of the Venetian and Florentine schools. The decoration, on a gold ground, is divided into concentric bands. In the center, around the opening of the lantern, are orna-

The inside of the Baptistry cupola.

mental motifs. Next comes the image of *Christ Surrounded by Seraphs and Hosts of Angels;* in the third band are *Scenes from Genesis* (from the Creation to the Flood); in the fourth the *Story of Joseph*; in the fifth, *Scenes from the Life of Christ*; and in the last, the *Life of the Baptist*. The apsidal zone is dominated by the colossal figure of *Christ* in the Last Judgement. On either side, in three overlapping bands are: *Angels Announcing the Judgement; the Virgin; the Baptist and the Apostles; the Resurrection of the Dead and the Division of the Blessed and the Damned*, with a terrifying representation of Hell.

GIOTTO'S BELL TOWER

Construction of this tower began in 1334 under the direction of Giotto after a fire had destroyed the old bell tower of Santa Reparata. Giotto died in 1337 when the base of the tower had been completed. He was succeeded by Andrea Pisano and Francesco Talenti who finished the work (although the spire that was part of the original plans was never built). The building is of remarkable grace and elegance. The structure lightens as it rises, becoming complex with marble insets and fine perforations. The bas-reliefs on the base (the originals are in the Museo dell'Opera del Duomo) were executed by Andrea Pisano and his workmen under the supervision of Giotto. Giotto's Bell Tower, is a wonderful example of Florentine Gothic architecture, characterized by verticality and marked solidity. The Florentines were so proud of their creation that they actually imprisoned a Veronese merchant for two months after he had boldly expressed his scepticism about the Commune's ability to complete such a costly undertaking. There was no lack of tributes, however: the Emperor Charles V thought it such a fine work that it deserved to be encased in glass.

THE CATHEDRAL

The construction of the cathedral, dedicated to Santa Maria del Fiore (St. Mary of the Flower), was begun by Arnolfo di Cambio in 1294 by order of the authorities and the citizenry. They wanted a cathedral that was not only bigger than the church of Santa Reparata, but that was also "greater and more magnificent", and that would surpass the cathedrals of rival Tuscan cities in both size and beauty.

Left: *Giotto's Bell Tower.*
Opposite page: *the Cathedral façade.*

The interior of the cathedral; below from the left: ***Funeral monument to Niccolò da Tolentino,*** frescoed by *Andrea del Castagno;*
Funeral monument to Giovanni Acuto (John Hawkwood), frescoed by *Paolo Uccello.*

The new cathedral was built around the old church, incorporating its simple structure and two bell towers. Santa Reparata was finally pulled down in 1375, but

the Florentines went on calling the new cathedral by its old name for such a long time that the authorities had to inflict heavy fines in order to enforce the use of the new name of Santa Maria del Fiore. The lower part of Santa Reparata, buried beneath the floor of the Duomo till quite recently, can now be seen by going down a staircase on the right nave. It contains remains of frescoes, sculptures and tombstones, including that of Filippo Brunelleschi. Much artwork was done over the centuries to embellish the cathedral which still looks

severe with its ogival arches and clustered pillars. On the inside of the façade is an enormous clock, made in 1443 and decorated with four heads of Prophets paint-

ed by Paolo Uccello. Also by Paolo Uccello is the fresco of the *Monument to Giovanni Acuto* (John Hawkwood) on the wall in the left aisle (1435), next to it is that of the *Monument to Niccolò da Tolentino* by Andrea del Castagno (1456). Above the large octagonal tribune is the dome by Brunelleschi. The inside of the dome is decorated with a fresco by Giorgio Vasari and Federico Zuccari (1552-79) depicting the *Last Judgement* in five concentric circles.

Over the high altar is a wooden *Crucifix* by Benedetto

Another interior view of the Cathedral; below, *the Crypt of Santa Reparata.*

da Maiano, and around it is the octagonal *choir* by Baccio Bandinelli (1555) decorated with bas-reliefs. Behind the altar, on the right is the **Old Sacristy** with an *Ascension* in terra-cotta by Luca della Robbia in the lunette over the entrance. Directly opposite, on the other side of the Tribune, is the **New Sacristy** with a fine bronze door by Luca della Robbia, Michelozzo and Maso di Bartolomeo (1445-69), the *Resurrection* in the lunette is also by Luca. In the chapel at the end of the apse is a bronze urn by Ghiberti containing the *relics of Saint Zanobius.*

SANTA REPARATA

The old Florentine cathedral was torn down in 1375 after it had been incorporated into the new one, Santa Maria del Fiore. The lower part, brought to light during excavations begun in 1966, was built to a basilica plan with three naves. The many relics of the church include pieces in marble, mosaics and frescoes (some executed while work was already proceeding on the cathedral). The countless tombstones bear witness to its role as a memorial to the city's glories. Brunelleschi's tomb was discovered there in 1972, it is believed that Arnolfo di Cambio and Giotto are also buried there.

THE CUPOLA

Filippo Brunelleschi was commissioned to build the cupola in 1418. At first, the distrustful authorities got Lorenzo Ghiberti to work with him. In order to get rid of his rival, Brunelleschi pretended to the ill and his colleague, who had no clear ideas about how to direct the work, was obliged to resign. The master's difficult temperament also affected his relations with the workmen. One day, irritated by a request for a rise in wages, he dismissed them all and then rehired them at half pay. Brunelleschi worked on the dome until his death. He often did not leave for days at a time, like the workmen for whom he organized canteens and hostelries inside the cupola to avoid frequent and tiresome climbs up and down.

The cathedral dome; below: *Cantoria,* by *Luca della Robbia* (detail); bottom right: *statue of Boniface VIII* by *Arnolfo di Cambio.*

MUSEO DELL'OPERA DEL DUOMO

This museum contains works from the Cathedral, the Bell Tower and the Baptistry. A room on the ground floor houses the sculptures from the first façade of the cathedral that was demolished in 1587 with a splendid *Virgin and Child* by Arnolfo di Cambio. The next room contains building materials and devices used by Brunelleschi when building the dome. Another small room has a collection of precious reliquaries. The famous *Pietà* by Michelangelo is on the mezzanine. On the floor above, the two *cantorie* by Donatello and Luca della Robbia; panels by Andrea Pisano from the Bell Tower, the *statues of John the Baptist, the Magdalen,* and *Abacuc* by Donatello, and the silver altar from the Baptistry, the work of several artists including Michelozzo, Verrocchio and Pollaiolo.

Left: *The Magdalen,* wooden statue by *Donatello;* right: *The Pietà,* by *Michelangelo* (1553).

THE PIETA' BY MICHELANGELO

This work, one of the master's last (1553), was in the cathedral for a long time, but had been sculpted by the artist for his tomb in Santa Maria Maggiore in Rome, a project that was never completed. This is perhaps the most dramatic of Michelangelo's four versions of the Pietà. Christ's lifeless body sags down at the center of the pyramid formed by the three figures supporting it:

the *Magdalen* on the left, with the expression of calm sorrow given by Tiberio Calcagni, the pupil who finished the work after the master's death; the *grieving Nicodemus,* whose face, according to Giorgio Vasari, is a self-portrait of Michelangelo; *Mary,* with her expressive power enhanced by the fact that she is roughhewn in Michelangelo's characteristic "unfinished" manner. Also by Calcagni is Christ's left arm that Michelangelo destroyed (like the missing leg) because he was dissatisfied with them.

PALAZZO MEDICI RICCARDI

Built for Cosimo the Elder in Via Larga (now Via Cavour) between 1444 and 1460 by the Florentine architect and sculptor, Michelozzo Michelozzi, this was the prototype of all Florentine Renaissance places. Majestic and elegant, it was filled with artworks commissioned by the Medici: the main branch of the family lived there until 1540. In 1655 the palace was sold to the Riccardi family; today is it the seat of the provincial government and the Prefecture, so it is often used for art exhibits and cultural events. Inside there is a fine porticoed courtyard that contains items from ancient Rome and various pieces of sculpture. One of the outstanding rooms is the **Chapel by Michelozzo** that can be reached via the first staircase on the right in the courtyard. Here are the renowned frescoes by Benozzo Gozzoli depicting the *Procession of the Magi* (1459-60) in which many famous people of the era, including Lorenzo the Magnificent, are portrayed.

The façade of the Palazzo Medici Riccardi;
below: ***Procession of the Magi*** by *Benozzo Gozzoli* (detail).

From the left: *Brunelleschi's cloister in San Lorenzo* and *the interior of the basilica.*

SAN LORENZO

An ancient basilica consecrated in 393 by St. Ambrose, bishop of Milan, this was probably the first church to be built in the city and was then outside the walls. It was rebuilt in the 11th century and then radically restored in the 15th century for the Medici as it was the family church. The spacious, light and elegant interior is one of the masterpieces of the early Florentine Renaissance. The work of Brunelleschi, it was designed in 1420 and he directed construction from 1442 until his death in 1446. It is in the shape of a Latin cross with three naves and side chapels. There are numerous masterpieces. These include two bronze *pulpits* by Donatello at the end of the central nave, his last work (c. 1400) that was completed by pupils after his death; a fine marble *tabernacle* by Desiderio da Settignano (mid 16th century) opposite the pulpit on the right; the *Marriage of the Virgin,* a painting by Rosso Fiorentino (1523); a remarkable *Annunciation* with *Scenes from the Life of St. Nicholas of Bari* by Filippo

Lippi (c. 1440) in the predella. Finally, there is the **Old Sacristy**, outstanding for its architecture and works of art, reached from the left transept. Elegant and of crystalline simplicity in its spatial conception, it fully expresses Brunelleschi's architectural ideals (1420-29). It is a chapel with a central plan, comprising a cube, surmounted by a half-dome, with gores, with all the edges in pietra serena against white plaster, a typically Brunelleschian decoration. The eight beautiful roundels in the lunettes and pendentives (4 with *Scenes from the Life of St. John the Evangelist* and 4 with the *Evangelists*) are by Donatello, as are the two bronze doors flanking the altar, and a fine terra-cotta *bust of St. Lawrence.* In the center of the chapel is the *tomb of Giovanni di Bicci dei Medici* and *Piccarda Bueri,* the parents of Cosimo the Elder by Andrea Cavalcanti (1434). On the left wall, under a large arch is the *tomb of Piero the Gouty and Giovanni dei Medici,* sons of Cosimo the Elder. The tomb was made by Andrea del Verrocchio who was perhaps helped by the young Leonardo da Vinci (1472).

The interior of the Chapel of the Princes;
below: *Day,* on the tomb of Giuliano dei Medici, by *Michelangelo.*

THE MEDICI CHAPELS

The impressive and lavish **Chapel of the Princes** was commissioned by Ferdinando I in 1602. Work began two years later to plans by Matteo Nigetti, who was assisted by Buontalenti, and continued for over a century. The large octagon is entirely covered with semi-precious stone inlays and the effect is spectacular. Against the walls are the sarcophagi of the six Medici grand dukes; above the tombs of Ferdinando I and Cosimo II there are gilded bronze statues by Ferdinando Tacca; below are the coats of arms of sixteen Tuscan cities, which are also inlaid in semi-precious stones. The inside of the dome is frescoed with *Scenes from the Old* and *New Testaments* by Pietro Benvenuti (1828). A cor-

ridor leads to the **New Sacristy**, the famous and beautiful chapel that Michelangelo built for Giulio dei Medici, later Pope Clement VII. It was Michelangelo's first experience in architecture. He worked on it through various vicissitudes from 1520 until 1534, but it was never completed. Built on a square plan, the chapel resembles the structure of Brunelleschi's Old Sacristy with ribbing in pietra serena on white plaster, but with much richer and complex architectural decoration (niches, windows, arches, etc.). Of the many planned tombs, the only ones completed were those of two minor members of the great Florentine family: *Giuliano,* Duke of Nemours and *Lorenzo,* Duke of Urbino. The two twin tombs are set against the splendid architecture: sculptures of the deceased are placed over the sarcophagi which are decorated with the famous allegorical statues.

22

The statues of Dusk (left) and *Dawn* (right);
below left: *Lorenzo, Duke of Urbino.*

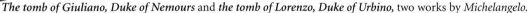

Giuliano is portrayed as an ancient warrior with armor and is sublimely idealized. On the tomb are the figures of *Night* reclining in sleep, and *Day*, muscular and vigorous with powerful, twisting legs and an unfinished face. Lorenzo is in a noble, meditative pose (he is also called "il Pensieroso") with a war helmet on his head. At his feet are the melancholy, dozing *Dusk* and the awakening *Dawn*, perhaps the most beautiful and famous of the four statues. In the back, above the tomb that contains the remains of Lorenzo the Magnificent and his brother Giuliano, killed by the Pazzi conspiracy, is the beautiful *Virgin and Child*, also by Michelangelo, between two sculptures by his pupils.

The tomb of Giuliano, Duke of Nemours and *the tomb of Lorenzo, Duke of Urbino,* two works by *Michelangelo.*

PIAZZA DELLA SIGNORIA

The Tribunal of the Guilds.

In Roman times the area that is now the center of the city was occupied by dwellings and the theater. At the end of the 13th century the area was included in the town-planning scheme directed by Arnolfo di Cambio who requisitioned and tore down the houses of the Ghibelline families and began to build Palazzo Vecchio. Henceforth the piazza became the stage for public speeches, ceremonies, meetings, riots and public executions. One of the most famous was that of Gerolamo Savonarola, the preacher who was briefly arbiter of public life and then excommunicated and burned at the stake on May 23, 1498; the spot is now indicated by a plaque. The piazza lacks unity owing to uncoordinated building that continued until the 19th century. The Gothic loggia was erected in the 14th century; a false Renaissance-style palace was built opposite Palazzo Vecchio in the 19th century. On the side opposite the Loggia, at n°5 is the **Alberto della Ragione collection** (works of contemporary Italian art), and at n°7, stands **Palazzo Uguccioni**, built to plans by Michelangelo or Raphael, and on the other side is the **Tribunal of the Guilds** (1359).

Aerial view of Piazza della Signoria.

THE NEPTUNE FOUNTAIN

Bartolomeo Ammannati was employed by Grand Duke Cosimo I on the recommendation of Vasari. He worked as an architect on rebuilding the Pitti Palace, the two bridges, Alla Carraia and Santa Trinità and the construction of many palaces in the city. As a sculptor his most important achievement is the fountain in the piazza, commissioned by Cosimo and executed between 1563 and 1576. In the center of the large polygonal pool is the large statue of *Neptune*; beneath the statue is a coach drawn by sea-horses. All around and at the edge of the pool are the magnificent bronze figures of *Naiads*, *Tritons* and *Satyrs*, that reveal the hand of Ammannati's assistant, Giambologna.

The Neptune Fountain by *Bartolomeo Ammannati;* left: *the statue of Neptune.*

THE LOGGIA DEI LANZI

The Loggia was built between 1376 and 1383 by Benci di Cione and Simone Talenti. It consists of three large, classical round arches on clustered columns that lead to a large cross-vaulted porch. Two heraldic lions flank the entrance: the one on the right dates from the Classical period, the other is from the sixteenth century. Under the right arch is the *Rape of the Sabine Women* by Giambologna (1583). The left arch frames the *Perseus* by Benvenuto Cellini (1546-54). The loggia also contains *Hercules and Nessus*, another group by Giambologna; *Menelaus with the Dying Patroclus,* a Roman copy of a 4th century B.C. original, and six Roman female statues.

Perseus by *Benvenuto Cellini;* left: *The Rape of the Sabine Women* by *Giambologna;* below: *the Loggia dei Lanzi.*

PALAZZO VECCHIO

Palazzo della Signoria, also known as Palazzo Vecchio, the old palace, since the mid 15th century when the Medici moved to the Pitti Palace, was the residence of the highest authorities in the city, her political center (it is still the seat of the municipal government), and a symbol of the strength and harmony of established institutions. The building was begun in 1299, and in all probability it was designed by the great architect Arnolfo di Cambio. The 94 meter high tower brilliantly positioned off-center to echo the asymmetry of the piazza, was completed in 1310. The palace was enlarged in 1343, in 1495 (by Cronaca) and then in the 16th century by Vasari (who redesigned the interior), Giovanni Battista del Tasso and Buontalenti. The interior of the palace, the rooms and artworks are enormously interesting. On the ground floor are the courtyard by Michelozzo and the Sala d'Arme, the only room that has not been changed. On the first floor: the Salone dei Cinquecento; the adjacent Study of Francesco I; the Sala dei Dugento and the Apartment of Leo X; the rooms of Leo X, Lorenzo the Magnificent and Cosimo I are open to the public. On the second floor there is the Room of the Elements, the Apartment of Eleonora de Toledo, the Chapel of the Signoria, the Audience Room, the Sala dei Gigli with the adjacent Room of the Maps and the Chancellery.

Left: *Palazzo Vecchio*; below: *the Salone dei Cinquecento.*

Piazzale degli Uffizi; right; *the Tribune;* below: *The Holy Family*
also known as the *"Tondo Doni"* by *Michelangelo* (c. 1504).

THE UFFIZI GALLERY

The Uffizi is not only the oldest art gallery in the world, it is the most important in Italy, and one of the greatest in Europe if not the whole world. The building housing the Gallery is itself splendid; it was built for Cosimo I in the mid 16th century between the Palazzo Vecchio and the Arno River to house public offices (hence the name which means "offices"). The planning was entrusted to Giorgio Vasari who built it between 1559 and the year of his death (1574). The highly original building stands over two long porticoes joined by a third side that opens onto the Arno with a magnificent, impressive arch. Work on the Uffizi was resumed in 1580 by order of Francesco I and directed by Bernardo Buontalenti who built the large Medici Theater (dismantled in 1890) and the famous Tribune. At the same time the top story of the loggia was rebuilt, the offices were transferred elsewhere, and some of the rooms were used to house collections of works or art, weapons and scientific curiosities: this is how the Gallery was born.

Allegory of Spring by *Sandro Botticelli* (c. 1482-83); below, from the left: *Madonna and Child with Two Angels* by *Filippo Lippi* (c. 1465) and *Portrait of Federico da Montefeltro* by *Piero della Francesca.*

The Birth of Venus by *Sandro Botticelli* (1484-86); below, left: *Madonna in Glory*, by *Giotto* and *Maestà* by *Duccio di Buoninsegna*.

The Battle of San Romano by *Paolo Uccello*; below: *Annunciation* by *Leonardo da Vinci* (c. 1470).

Two views of the Ponte Vecchio (above and below); bottom right: ***bust of Benvenuto Cellini*** by *Romanelli* (1900).

PONTE VECCHIO

A s the name implies (Old Bridge), this is the oldest bridge in Florence. It has existed since the days of the Roman colony when the piers were made of stone and the surface of wood. Destroyed by flood in 1117, it was completely rebuilt in stone but collapsed again in the terrible flood of November 4, 1333. It was rebuilt for the last time in 1345 (perhaps by the painter architect Taddeo Gaddi) with three spans, and very wide, planned with room for shops on either side. Initially there were butcher shops, later came the grocers, smiths, shoemakers, etc. They built the characteristic little back-rooms that project over the river, resting on supports and brackets. In 1519, however, Ferdinando I evicted them all, granting the shops to goldsmiths only. Since then the bridge has been almost like a single display window filled with precious stones, interrupted only by the two terraces in the middle. In the one facing downstream there is a *bust of Benvenuto Cellini* master goldsmith, by Raffaello Romanelli (1900).

Pitti Palace; below: *The Madonna of the Chair* by *Raphael.*

Opposite page, top left: *La Velata* by *Raphael;* right: *Portrait of Agnolo Doni* by *Raphael* (1505); bottom: *The Three Ages of Man, Venetian school* (XVI century).

PITTI PALACE

Towards the middle of the 15th century Luca Pitti, a member of rich merchant family, decided that his prestige would be proved if he could have a home that was even more beautiful than the one Michelozzo was building for the Medici. He selected the site on the Boboli Hill and commissioned Brunelleschi to draw up the plans that were submitted around 1445. Work began in 1457, after the master's death, under the direction of Luca Fancelli, one of Filippo's pupils. The façade overlooking the piazza consisted only of the seven central windows; the three stories were separated by slender balconies and faced with rusticated stone. When Luca Pitti died in 1473 the palace was still unfinished. Then the Pitti family fell into disfavor, and the work was continued by the Medici themselves, specifically by Eleonora di Toledo, wife of Cosimo I who bought the building and the land behind it in 1549. In the 16th and 17th centuries this became the Medici's palace; they enlarged it, created the gardens on the Boboli hill, and lengthened the building to nine windows on each side.

THE PALATINE GALLERY

The idea for the collection dates back to the last two Medici, Cosimo II and Ferdinando II who commissioned a great Baroque painter, Pietro da Cortona to fresco some of the rooms on the piano nobile of the Pitti Palace with mythological subjects celebrating the glories of the house of Medici (1641-47). Ferdinando began to arrange pictures in these rooms, creating a new family collection to complement the existing one in the Uffizi.

The Lorraine dynasty continued both with the decoration of the rooms and the art collection. In 1828 Grand Duke Peter Leopold opened the museum to the public. Limited at first to the five rooms of Venus, Apollo, Mars, Jupiter and Saturn, the collection grew to its present size in 1928 when a great number of paintings were exchanged with the Uffizi, and many 16th and 17th century works by Italian and foreign painters were acquired.

THE BOBOLI GARDENS

Work on creating the gardens on the Boboli hill began at the same time as the rebuilding of the Pitti Palace. Near the entrance is the *Bacchus Fountain*, in which Valerio Cioli portrayed a dwarf from the court of Cosimo I astride a tortoise; further on is the *Grotto by Buontalenti* built between 1583 and 1588 for the extravagant Francesco I. Going on,

one comes to the *Amphitheater* that was originally grass in the 16th century and later rebuilt in the 18th. Continuing on to the left one comes to the *Neptune Fountain* and the *Giardino del Cavaliere*, where the Porcelain Museum is situated; or going straight ahead, along a wide path, the *Viottolone*, one reaches the *Piazzale dell'Isolotto*, with its large pool and lush island with lemon trees and the *Oceanus Fountain* by Giambologna.

Top: *detail of Buontalenti's Grotto*; opposite: *the Pitti Palace seen from the Boboli Gardens*; below, left: *the Viottolone*; right: *the Fountain of Oceanus* by *Giambologna*.

The church of Santo Spirito, on the square of the same name; right: *the interior.*

SANTO SPIRITO

The church of Santo Spirito stands on the left bank of the Arno in one of the city's working class districts. The original plans were drawn by Filippo Brunelleschi in 1444. The interior was executed by Antonio Manetti and other pupils after the master's death, while the simple façade dates from the 17th century. The Baroque high altar, an elaborate structure by Giovanni Caccini (1608), stands in the center of the presbytery. In the right transept there is a fine *Virgin and Child with Saints and Patrons* by Filippo Lippi (c. 1490). In the apse is a polyptych by Maso di Banco of the *Virgin and Child with Saints*; on a nearby altar is a painting of the *Holy Martyrs* by Alessandro Allori (1574). The **Corbinelli Chapel**, an elegant piece of sculpture and architecture by Andrea Sansovino, is in the left transept.

The church of Santa Maria del Carmine.

SANTA MARIA DEL CARMINE

The unfinished façade is a high, severe wall of rough stone. The interior is prevalently 18th century. At the end of the right transept is the **Brancacci Chapel**: the frescoes by Masaccio and Masolino (1425-28) marked a turning point in the history of Western art. There are two cycles of illustrations on the walls of the chapel: *The Original Sin* and *Scenes from the Life of St. Peter.* The most significant scenes are *The Expulsion*, a powerful masterpiece by Masaccio that faces the *Temptation of Adam and Eve* by Masolino on the opposite wall. The *Resurrection of Tabitha* is an example of how well the two artists worked together; *Baptism of the Neophytes* was done by Masaccio alone, as was *The Tribute Money.*

Preceding page: *the Brancacci Chapel.*
Above, from left to right: ***The Expulsion*** by *Masaccio* and ***the Temptation of Adam and Eve***
by *Masolino*; below: ***The Tribute Money*** by *Masaccio.*

SANTA TRINITÀ

The church of Santa Trinità dates back to the 11th century; the Mannerist façade was designed by Buontalenti (1593-94). The interior is rich in works of art that include a magnificently frescoed chapel (fourth on the right) with a panel painting by Lorenzo Monaco (1420-25); a *Magdalen* in wood by Desiderio da Settignano (1464, fifth chapel on the left); the famous **Sassetti Chapel** (right transept); the *tomb of Benozzo Federighi,* a masterpiece by Luca della Robbia (c. 1450, left transept); and finally, in the sacristy, the Renaissance *tomb of Onofrio Strozzi* by Piero di Niccolò Lamberti (1421).

The church stands on the piazza of the same name and is surrounded by fine buildings such as the **Palazzo Spini-Ferroni** and the **Palazzo Bartolini-Salimbeni** a masterpiece by Baccio d'Agnolo. In the middle of the piazza is a tall column that supports the *statue of Justice* by Francesco del Tadda (1581).

The church of Santa Trinità

Palazzo Strozzi.

PALAZZO STROZZI

Filippo Strozzi, a Florentine merchant of long-standing wealth commissioned Benedetto da Maiano to build the palace in 1489. Benedetto was succeeded by Cronaca who directed the work until 1504. Construction was interrupted and resumed several times. The Strozzi family fell into disfavor in 1538 and the palace was confiscated by Cosimo I dei Medici and was returned 30 years later. The massive building (which many consider to be the finest private building of the Renaissance) has a stone plinth that runs along the entire base, projecting like a bench. The exterior resembles the Palazzo Medici-Riccardi with pronounced rustication. At the top is a magnificent cornice by Cronaca; the two upper stories have fine double-lighted windows. The majestic internal courtyard with a columned portico and loggia was also designed by Cronaca.

The church of Santa Maria Novella on the square of the same name; right: *the interior;*
below: ***The Trinity*** detail of the fresco by *Masaccio* (c. 1427).

SANTA MARIA NOVELLA

This great Dominican church stands on the site of a 10th century country oratory. Construction was begun in 1246, and the first architects were Fra Sisto and Fra Ristoro. The façade was begun in 1300, and the lower part was finished before the middle of the century in the typically Florentine Romanesque-Gothic style. After the middle of the 15th century Leon Battista Alberti, the great architectural theorist of the Quattrocento, completed the inlaid marble façade by adding the central doorway and the upper part, of extraordinary elegance, with round window, tympanum and lateral scrolls. The interior shows the influence of Cistercian Gothic in the "softened" form that this style developed in Italy: it is a Latin cross with three naves and clustered columns. An incredible number of artworks decorate the walls and chapels. In the second bay on the right aisle is *the tomb of the Blessed Villana* by Bernardo Rossellino (1451). The right transept leads to the **Ruccellai Chapel:** on the altar is a *Madonna* by Nino Pisano; the *tombstone of Leonardo Dati* by Ghiberti (1425) is sunken into the floor. The **Chapel of Filippo Strozzi** (to the right of the main altar) is entirely covered with frescoes by Filippo Lippi (c. 1500) portraying *Scenes from the Lives of St. John and St. Philip*; the *tomb of Filippo Strozzi* is by Benedetto da Maiano (1493). The **Main Chapel**

has frescoes by Domenico Ghirlandaio (c. 1495: his helpers probably included the young Michelangelo), with beautiful *Scenes from the Life of the Virgin.* The **Gondi Chapel** (on the left of the main chapel) has the famous *Crucifix* by Brunelleschi, the only sculpture by the master that has survived to this day. In the **Strozzi Chapel** (left transept) there are frescoes by Nardo di Cione (c. 1367); a remarkable representation of *Hell*. In the sacristy nearby is a *Crucifix* by the young Giotto. And finally, in the third bay on the left aisle is the marvelous *Trinity* by Masaccio (c. 1427) and the *pulpit* designed by Brunelleschi.

On this page: *Scenes from the Life of the Virgin* frescoes by *Ghirlandaio* in the main chapel (details).

On this page: *three details of the frescoes in the Spagnoli Chapel* by *Andrea di Bonaiuto*;
from the left: *Preaching, Resurrection* (detail) and *Ascent to the Calvary* (below).

A room in the Accademia Gallery with the Rape of the Sabine Women by *Giambologna;* right: *"The Tribune"* by *Emilio de Fabris* (1882); below: three works by *Michelangelo: the Palestrina Pietà* (left), **The Young Slave** (center); **The Bearded Slave** (right).

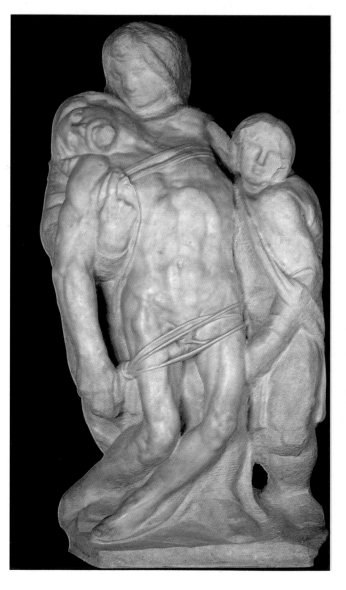

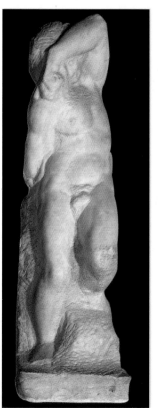

THE ACCADEMIA GALLERY

This is one of the most renowned galleries in Italy, visited by thousands of people, mainly because of the *David* and other famous statues by Michelangelo. There is also an outstanding collection of paintings from the 13th to the 16th century.

On this page: three works by *Michelangelo*.
Above, from the left: *The Prisoner or Atlas* and *the Young Desantesi*;
opposite: *The David.*

THE DAVID BY MICHELANGELO

This famous statue, perhaps the most famous sculpture in Western art, was carved between 1501 and April 1504, a month after Michelangelo's 29th birthday. In June of the same year, 1504, a committee of distinguished artists decided to place the splendid and already greatly admired statue on the steps outside Palazzo Vecchio as if to symbolize and defend republican liberty. In fact, the David symbolized the two civil virtues of fortitude (in the harmonious yet powerful body, static on the right, with the hand clutching the stone, while the left leg is extended and the arm with the sling bends), and Anger (in the watchful, resolute face). In 1527, during a riot, the left arm was broken off by a bench that had been hurled from a palace window. Giorgio Vasari picked up the three pieces and the restorations were done in 1543. In 1873 the David was taken to the Accademia and a copy was placed on the steps. The grandiose nature of the piece (the statue alone, without the base is over 13 feet high); the dramatic tension; the proud and beautiful face confidently gazing at his adversary; the anatomical precision with muscles tensed, ready to spring; the superb moral dignity of the character embody the youthful vision of Michelangelo, who surrounds the Biblical champion with an aura of heroism.

SAN MARCO

The church and adjacent **Monastery of San Marco** stand on one side of the square with the same name. The 16th century-style façade was actually constructed in the late 18th century. The interior, remodeled by Giambologna in 1588 and by Silvani in 1678 contains fine artworks including a beautiful *Crucifix* from Giotto's school, and in the third chapel on the right an 8th century mosaic of the *Virgin at Prayer*.

THE MUSEUM OF SAN MARCO

The entrance to the monastery of San Marco is next to the church. This was one of the nerve centers of fifteenth century Florence thanks to the favor it held with Cosimo the Elder and Lorenzo the Magnificent, the unquestioned authority of the prior St. Antonius and the fact that it had hosted Savonarola, Beato Angelico and Fra' Bartolomeo. Fra Angelico was one of the greatest artists of the 15th century. He infused the new, robust shapes inherited from Masaccio with a still Gothic spirit to express a mystical, contemplative religious experience. The **Cloister of St. Antonius** by Michelozzo has frescoed lunettes, and there are some interesting rooms opening on to it. The **Pilgrims' Hospice** houses an exceptional series of panel paintings by Fra Angelico: the *Linen Makers' Tabernacle*, the altarpiece from the Bosco ai Frati, the *Annalena Altarpiece*, the *Deposition*, and the *Last Judgement*. The **Chapter Room** contains the splendid *Crucifixion* by Beato Angelico. The same artist also decorated the **Dormitory** on the first floor between 1439 and 1445; the series of cells has such masterpieces as the *Annunciation*, *Noli me tangere*, the *Transfiguration*, and the *Coronation of the Virgin*. In the **Prior's room** there is a *Portrait of Savonarola* (who lived there), painted by a pupil of Fra' Bartolomeo.

*The church of San Marco; below: **St. Dominic at the foot of the Crucifix** by Beato Angelico; right: **Noli me Tangere** by Beato Angelico.*

Annunciation by *Beato Angelico;* below: *Last Supper* by *Domenico Ghirlandaio.*

SANTISSIMA ANNUNZIATA

In 1250 seven young Florentines, later beatified as the Seven Saints, founded the order of the Servites, or Servants of Mary and began to build a shrine dedicated to the Virgin. The church was rebuilt by Michelozzo in the 15th century, and then by Antonio Manetti who, with the cooperation of Leon Battista Alberti, completed the design of the circular Tribune at the end of the single nave. The portico on the piazza is late 16th century. Between this and the church there is the **Cloister of the Vows** with fine early 16th century frescoes by Andrea del Sarto, Pontormo, Rosselli, Franciabigio and other Mannerists. Inside the church there is a highly venerated 14th century Florentine school *Annunciation* which legend attributed to the hand of an angel. Among the many works of art mention should be made of two *lecterns* in the form of eagles (English, 15th century); in the elegant Tribune, Jesus and *St. Julian* by Andrea del Castagno (c. 1455, first chapel on the left) and the *Trinity* by the same artist (second chapel on the left).

Above, left: *monument to the Grand Duke Ferdinando I* by *Tacca* (1608);
right: *marble temple* by *Michelozzo*, containing *The Annunciation*, Florentine school (XIV century);
below: *the church of Santissima Annunziata.*

THE SPEDALE DEGLI INNOCENTI

In 1419 the Guild of Silk Merchants decided to purchase land and build a foundling hospital. Brunelleschi was commissioned to draw up the plans, and the work was completed in 1457. The façade comprises nine wide arches on columns that stand at the top of a flight of steps. Above these, a low upper story has tympanum windows, and between the arches are glazed terra-cotta tondi by Andrea della Robbia (c. 1487). Inside there are two extraordinary cloisters by Brunelleschi and a Gallery containing mostly 15th century art. The main paintings in the collection include an *Annunciation* by Giovanni del Biondo; the *Virgin and Child with Saints* by Piero di Cosimo; the *Adoration of the Magi* by Ghirlandaio (1488); a *Virgin and Child with Angels* from the school of Perugino; the *Madonna of the Innocents* attributed to Pontormo, and a *St. Sebastian* by Andrea del Sarto.

The cloister of the Spedale degli Innocenti by *Filippo Brunelleschi*, below: *the Spedale degli Innocenti.*

THE ARCHEOLOGICAL MUSEUM

The museum is divided into three sections: the Etrurian Topographical Museum, the Etruscan-Greco-Roman Antiquities and the Egyptian Collection. On the ground floor some of the rooms are specifically arranged for educational purposes, here are the famous François vase and the *Mater Matuta*. The pleasant garden contains reconstructions, made partly with authentic materials, of funeral monuments and Etruscan tombs. The Egyptian Collection is on the first floor. The most interesting exhibits include: the *statue of Thutmose III* (1490-1436 B.C.), the *"Fayyum" portrait of a woman* (II century A.D.), sarcophagi, mummies and a war chariot. Among the antiquities on the first floor there are also Attic kouroi from the 6th century B.C.; Etruscan funeral urns; the *statue of the Orator* (c. 100 B.C.); Etruscan sarcophagi; the *Chimera of Arezzo*; the *small Idol*; Attic vases and Etruscan bucchero.

Above left: *the François Vase* signed by the potter *Ergotimos* and the painter *Kleitias*; right: *an Egyptian stele;* below, left: *Mater Matuta*, Etruscan sculpture (second half of the V century B.C.); top right: *wooden figurine* (Egypt, c. 2400 B.C.); and *the sarcophagus of Larthia Seianti* (II century B.C.).

THE BARGELLO MUSEUM

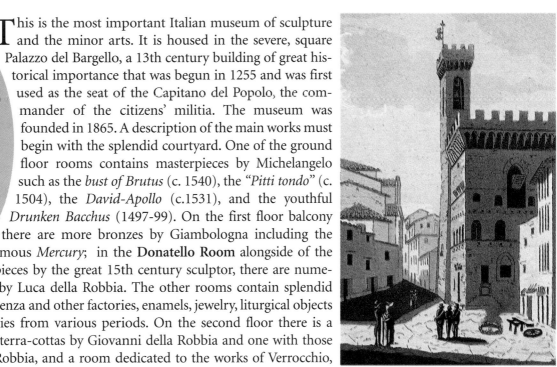

This is the most important Italian museum of sculpture and the minor arts. It is housed in the severe, square Palazzo del Bargello, a 13th century building of great historical importance that was begun in 1255 and was first used as the seat of the Capitano del Popolo, the commander of the citizens' militia. The museum was founded in 1865. A description of the main works must begin with the splendid courtyard. One of the ground floor rooms contains masterpieces by Michelangelo such as the *bust of Brutus* (c. 1540), the *"Pitti tondo"* (c. 1504), the *David-Apollo* (c.1531), and the youthful *Drunken Bacchus* (1497-99). On the first floor balcony there are more bronzes by Giambologna including the famous *Mercury*; in the **Donatello Room** alongside of the masterpieces by the great 15th century sculptor, there are numerous terra-cottas by Luca della Robbia. The other rooms contain splendid majolicas from Faenza and other factories, enamels, jewelry, liturgical objects and valuable ivories from various periods. On the second floor there is a room containing terra-cottas by Giovanni della Robbia and one with those by Andrea della Robbia, and a room dedicated to the works of Verrocchio, Rossellino and Pollaiolo.

Above, left: *David* by *Donatello* (c. 1430); above, right: *the Bargello "Prison"* in a nineteenth century print; below, left: *Bust of Brutus* by Michelangelo Buonarotti and *Mercury* by Giambologna.

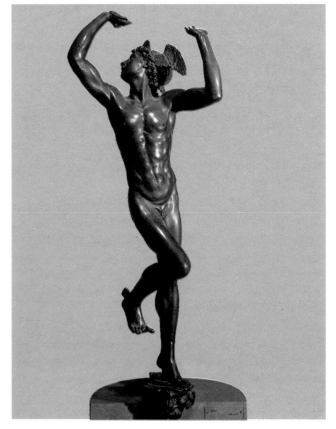

The church of Santa Croce on the square of the same name, below: *Painted cross in the Main Chapel* by the *Maestro di Figline* who may have been *Giovanni di Bonino.*

SANTA CROCE

In 1294 Arnolfo di Cambio began the construction of the basilica, in the simple, yet monumental form typical of Franciscan churches. The church was consecrated in 1443 in the presence of Pope Eugenius IV. In 1566 Giorgio Vasari was commissioned by Cosimo I to build some altars in the lateral naves, this involved destroying the old choir and many frescoes. The façade was only done in the mid 19th century to a design by Nicolò Matas, in a neo-Gothic style, like the bell tower by Gaetano Baccani (1847). The interior has three naves with pointed arches supported on octagonal stone pillars. There are no fewer than 276 grave markers set into the floor (the oldest is from the 14th century). In the central nave, at the third pillar on the right is the fine *pulpit* by Benedetto da Maiano (1472-76); the reliefs on the panels portray *Scenes from the Life of St. Francis.* In the right nave, at the first pillar there is the *Madonna of the Milk* by Rossellino (1478); opposite is the *funeral monument to Michelangelo* by Vasari and his helpers (1570). In the right transept is the **Castellani Chapel** frescoed by Agnolo Gaddi around 1385. The frescoes depict *Scenes from the Life of St. Nicholas of Bari, John the Baptist and Anthony Abbot.* At the end of the transept is the entrance to the **Baroncelli Chapel** frescoed with *Scenes from the Life of the Virgin* by Taddeo Gaddi, and on the altar there is a polyptych with the *Coronation of the Virgin* from Giotto's workshop. The **Peruzzi Chapel** has splendid frescoes by Giotto with *Scenes from the Life of St. John the Baptist* and *St. John the Evangelist*. The **Bardi Chapel** is decorated with *Scenes from the Life of St. Francis* also by Giotto and this cycle should be considered among the painter's masterpieces (c.1325). The **Chapel of the High Altar** has frescoes by Agnolo Gaddi and a *polyptych* by Niccolò Gaddi (late 14th century). The **Bardi di Vernio Chapel** has fine *Scenes from the Life of St. Sylvester* by Maso di Banco (c. 1340). The **Bardi Chapel** at the end of the transept has a *Crucifix* by Donatello (c. 1425). On the left is the **Salviati Chapel** with the nineteenth century *tomb of Sofia Zamoyski* by Lorenzo Bartolini. There is yet another series of funeral monuments in the left nave including the *tomb of Galileo Galilei* by Giulio Foggini (1737) and the *tomb of Carlo Marsuppini* by Desiderio da Settignano.

Right: *the interior of Santa Croce*; below: *the Baroncelli Chapel* with frescoes depicting *Scenes from the Life of the Virgin* by *Taddeo Gaddi* (1332-38), Giotto's main pupil. The polyptych in the chapel has also been attributed to him.
Below, right: *the left transept.*

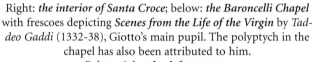

51

THE MAIN CHAPEL IN SANTA CROCE

The great 14th century polyptych on the altar portrays the *Madonna and Saints* and was done by Niccolò Gerini, the *Crucifix* above is by the Maestro di Figline (first half of the 14th century). In the vault of the choir behind the altar are *Christ, St. Francis* and the *Evangelists* by Agnolo Gaddi. The same Gaddi, Giotto's pupil and colleague (whose workshop he inherited) also painted the complex and crowded scenes of the *Legend of the Cross* in a style that is not lacking in naturalistic vigor. The Legend of the Cross tells the story of the wood with which the cross was made: *St. Michael gives Seth a branch of the Tree of Knowledge; Seth plants the branch on Adam's grave; the tree is used to make a bridge which is then buried by Solomon; the Israelites dig it up to make a cross; St. Helena finds the Cross; Khosrow, king of the Persians, steals it; finally, the Byzantine king, Heraclius is warned in a vision and having defeated Khosrow brings the Cross back to the Holy City.*

Detail of the remains of the frescoes in the Bardi Chapel, dedicated to the Life of St. Francis, by *Giotto* (1320-25); below: *Funeral monument to Michelangelo Buonarroti* designed by *Vasari* (1570); right: *monument to Dante Alighieri* by *Stefano Ricci* (1829).

The courtyard of the Pazzi Chapel.

THE PAZZI CHAPEL

Filippo Brunelleschi designed the building and began work around 1430. He worked on it at intervals until 1444; then other architects completed the building. In front of the entrance there is a pronaos with six Corinthian columns and a wide central arch between pietra serena panels.The frieze with cherubs' heads was done by Desiderio da Settignano. The chapel has a dome with a conical covering (1461). Under the portico is another small dome in colored terra-cotta by Luca della Robbia who also executed the tondo of *St. Andrew* above the beautifully carved door by Giuliano da Maiano (1472). Inside the walls are white with fluted pietra serena pilaster strips and wide arches. The only touches of color come from the tondos by Luca della Robbia depicting the *Apostles* and the *Evangelists*.

CASA BUONARROTI

Having revealed his artistic talents at a very young age, Michelangelo was received into the circle of artists patronized by Lorenzo the Magnificent when he was only 14, and studied the Magnificent's splendid collection of ancient statues. Michelangelo's earliest known works exhibited in Casa Buonarroti date from that period. These include the The *Madonna of the Stairs* (c. 1490) in which the young artist revived the "flattened" bas-relief technique typical of Donatello. The *Battle of the Centaurs* (1492) is indicative of the future developments in Michelangelo's art (note the dramatic tension of the bodies and the "unfinished" technique). There is also a very fine wooden *Crucifixion* in which the delicate figure reveals the artist's intensive studies of anatomy during that period (c. 1493).

THE SYNAGOGUE

The Jewish synagogue on Via Farini was designed by the architects Vincenzo Micheli, Mariano Falcini and Marco Treves between 1872 and 1874. The eclectic trends in the architecture of the period are revealed in the combination of typically Florentine decorations (the two-colored bands) and Eastern elements (the Moorish arch). The impressive interior is richly decorated with mosaics of Venetian-Middle Eastern characters that are rigorously aniconic - there are no real images except for the symbols of the menorah, the *Star of David* and the *Tables of the Law*, in accordance with the dictates of the Jewish religion.

SAN MINIATO AL MONTE

This, one of the most beautiful and oldest churches in Florence, stands on the site of the city's earliest Christian settlements: the old Mons Florentinus where the woods were full of catacombs, then oratories and little hovels where monks lived. An oratory was dedicated to St. Miniato who was martyred on the hill in the 4th century. The Romanesque church was built over the site between the 11th-13th century. The façade is covered with marble in two colors, in a clear, solemn pattern. The fine central mosaic (13th century, heavily restored) portrays *Christ between the Virgin and St. Miniato*. At the top of the tympanum, there is an *Eagle* symbol of the Guild of Wool Merchants who had to guarantee the upkeep of the church. The interior has three naves, with a crypt and a presbytery above it. The floor of the nave is set with splendid slabs of inlaid marble. In the center, between the two flights of steps leading up to the presbytery is the **Chapel of the Crucifix** by Michelozzo (1448), commissioned by Piero the Gouty. The coffered ceiling is by Luca della Robbia, and on the end wall there are panel paintings by Agnolo Gaddi. From the left nave one enters the **Chapel of the Cardinal of Portugal**, one of the most elegant achievements of the Florentine Renaissance, built by Antonio Manetti (1461-66). The ceiling of the crypt above the altar is decorated with frescoes of the *Saints and Prophets* by Taddeo Gaddi (14th century).

From the top: *the Synagogue; Forte di Belvedere; the church of San Miniato.*

The city from Piazzale Michelangelo; right: *the monument to Michelangelo at the Piazzale.*

PIAZZALE MICHELANGELO

This is a large, panoramic terrace that affords a view of the whole city and the surrounding hills. It was conceived by Giuseppe Poggi in 1860. In the center is a *monument to Michelangelo* erected in 1875 with bronze copies of some of his marble sculptures.

FIESOLE

This charming little town about 6 km from Florence was founded by the Etruscans in the IV century B.C. and conquered by the Romans three centuries later. After the fall of the Empire it was an important bishopric, however, it succumbed to its stronger neighbor, Florence, in the 12th century. The center of the town is **Piazza Mino** where the main public buildings are. The cathedral, built in 1028, was modified in later years. The nearby **Museo Bandini** has interesting Della Robbia terra-cottas, works by Agnolo and Taddeo Gaddi and Lorenzo Monaco. The **Palazzo Pretorio** (15th century) also stands in Piazza Mino, with its façade and loggia decorated with coats of arms. From the Piazza it is just a short walk to the **Roman Amphitheater.** Near the amphitheater are the ruins of a temple (first Etruscan, later Roman) and the Roman baths. The **Archeological Museum** which is adjacent to the excavations contains Etruscan and Roman relics.

Top, left: *Piazza Mino da Fiesole;* right: *the street leading to San Francesco* on the hill of the same name; opposite: *the Roman amphitheater* (I century B.C.)

PISA

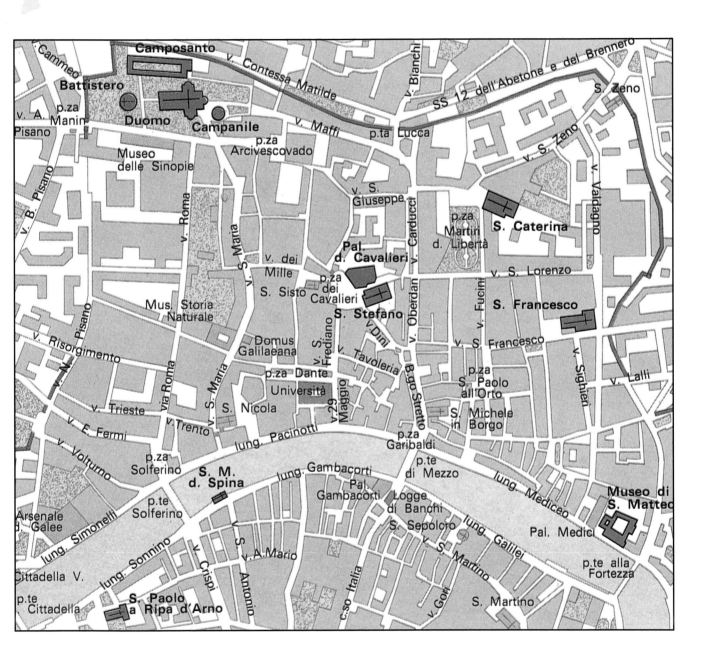

*P*isa, an important port in Roman times, extended its trade during the Middle Ages to become one of the great maritime republics in the Mediterranean. In the 11th century it wrested control of Sardinia, the start of a political and artistic influence not to be relinquished for centuries. The 11th and 12th centuries were also the peri-od in which the "Pisan" style in architecture and sculp-ture began to spread. Great building projects were begun such as the Campo dei Miracoli, and Giovanni Pisano imposed his new "manner" of sculpting on Tuscan art. Pisa's power over the seas was greatly diminished when it suffered a terrible defeat in 1284 at the hands of the

Genoese at the battle of Meloria. It marked the beginning of a long period of decline which, in turn, led to complete political dependence on Florence from 1406 on. The following years, however, saw a marked economic and cultural recovery, the port was enlarged and an important university was established. The bombings the city suffered during World War II caused severe damage to its artistic heritage, which was painstakingly restored so that it can now be admired in all its beauty by scholars and visitors from all over the world.

Aerial view of Piazza del Duomo.

PIAZZA DEL DUOMO

The visitor arriving here immediately understands why this is also called **Piazza dei Miracoli** (Square of Miracles). There can be few places in the world which have an effect comparable to that produced by the miraculous beauty of the architectural masterpieces which stand here: the cathedral, the Leaning Tower, the Baptistry and the Monumental Cemetery.

The buildings are surrounded by green lawns and in the background is the battlemented wall built under the consul Griffi in the 12th century. At the southern end of the square is a beautiful *fountain* dating from the 17th century. It is decorated with three splendid *putti* supporting Pisa's coat of arms. The monuments in the square were built from the 11th to the 14th century.

The cathedral and the Leaning Tower.

THE CATHEDRAL

The designer and builder of the cathedral was Buscheto whose tomb is located in the last blind arch of the façade to the left, in a classical strigilate sarcophagus. The once poorly interpreted inscription gave rise to a long lasting belief that Buscheto was of Greek origin, but the comparison it draws between the architect, Daedalus and Ulysses is simply meant to emphasize the merits and ingenuity of the creator of this wonderful building. Another inscription nearby reads: "Non habet exemeplum niveo de marmore templum - nowhere in the world is there such a temple made of pure white marble". Whoever composed this and the other verses carved into the marble fully appreciated the architectural beauty of this unique church, well situated not far from the city walls as it was then, and recognized that Pisa possesses a work of art that was and is unique in the world. Nor is this enthusiastic appreciation surprising when one looks at the structure of the temple which rises to dominate an ample space where, with other monuments, it seems to live and breath in its singular setting. Among the inscriptions to be found on the two blind arches to the left

façade that are meant to glorify the maritime enterprises of the Pisan Republic against the Saracens in the Mediterranean, to commemorate her victories and conquests, and to praise the heroism of her sailors in expanding her powers and riches during the 11th and 12th centuries, there is one that recalls the victorious Pisan expedition against the Saracens of Palermo. After this victory on August 6, 1063, the Pisans began construction of their cathedral dedicated to the Blessed Virgin, in appreciation of the help they had received. Buscheto completed his design which was to undergo some changes as can be seen in the sections that were built later. This is, of course, understandable in such a grandiose building: work continued for centuries, so it was affected by changes in tastes and the times, and the amount of money available for its completion. However, the original architect's plans were largely followed as is evident from an analysis of the building today. It is clearly Romanesque and, as such, the foundation and model of a noteworthy current in architectural style. This style, embodied by the cathedral, spread to influence not only other religious buildings erected in Pisa during the 12th, 13th and 14th centuries, and the surrounding countryside (albeit with certain modifications and limitations) but also to the religious buildings of many other Tuscan cities, the islands of the nearby archipelago, of Corsica and Sardinia and even as far as Dalmatia and Apulia. The vitality of the Pisan-Romanesque style, with its clarity of building formulae and well defined taste is proof of the city's political and commercial interests and dominant role. The remarkable diffusion of Pisan architectural style at the height of prosperity, attests to the republic's farreaching commercial and cultural influence.

Buscheto's cathedral is a basilica, in the shape of a Latin cross with five naves on the longitudinal arm and a transept with three naves separated by rows of big columns. This building, which is unique among contemporary structures, has spatial qualities that closely resemble early Christian churches in Rome. There is still some argument about how far the present form corresponds to Buscheto's designs since there is clear evidence of departures from the original plans. The cupola, supported by pillars at the junction of the two arms (added later, according to some critics); the transept which is lower than the central body of the church; the façade and the main apse, to name the major points of interest, offer ample material for discussion in the as yet unresolved issue of determining the dates of these changes and the artists responsible for them. These and other changes that can be seen inside are not, however, dissonant with the basic design, rather they are well integrated into the stylistic unity of the whole.

The transept and apse of the Cathedral.

The Cathedral façade.

THE FAÇADE

The façade of the cathedral was built by Rainaldo, Buscheto's successor, in the second half of the 13th century. Above and to the right of the main doors is the clearly legible Latin epigraph: "Rainaldus prudens operator..." The mosaics on the lunette were made by Alessio Baldovinetti in 1467 and restored in 1829. The central mosaic portrays the *Assumption of the Virgin*, the one on the left, *Saint Reparata*, and on the right, *St. John the Baptist*. Two beautiful classical columns flank the central door. Blind arches, lozenges and rosettes of Oriental inspiration can seen on the lower part of the façade. The upper part repeats the style of the Lombard arcade, a dominant theme in the architecture of the Leaning Tower and the main apse of the church. The four stories of the arcades diminish as they ascend, creating a perspective fugue of little arches and columns suggestive of the spectacular harmonics of contrapuntal music. High up on the right, in the second gallery, there is a small, red Oriental porphyry column. It was brought to Pisa from Majorca. According to a charming old legend it seems that whoever looks upon it will not be betrayed in love for at least one day.

THE DOOR OF ST. RANIERI

When Bonanno Pisano was forced to abandon work on the Leaning Tower, he turned his attention to sculpting the set of four wonderful portals for the Cathedral. Three façade doors were completely destroyed in the 1595 fire, whereas the fourth, named for **St. Ranieri**, since it opens onto the chapel dedicated to the saint, survived and is still in excellent condition today. The work is of great artistic value, filled with poetry and purity. Byzantine influence is strong in the severe, ascetic looking figures on the panels. The twenty panels depict *Scenes from the Life of Christ* in a simple, vigorous style. In the panels showing The *Nativity*, the *Flight into Egypt* and the *Crucifixion* it is easy to pick out the humanity, poetic sense and drama that foreshadowed the realistic feeling which characterized the second Medieval period in Italian sculpture.

The Door of St. Ranieri by *Bonanno Pisano;* above, right: *detail of one of the panels with Scenes from the Life of Christ.*

THE INTERIOR - The double aisles of the stately interior are marked by plain granite columns with Corinthian capitals. The upper galleries on either side of the nave, called matronei, were reserved for female worshippers. The striped marble facing repeats the pattern of the exterior decoration and adds a lively touch of color to the solemn procession of arches along the aisles and matronei. Towering over the junction of the transept and nave is the dome which rests upon pointed, Arabian style arches. The interior of the cathedral is embellished by remarkable artworks. In the center of the nave is a 16th century chandelier, popularly known as *Galileo's Lamp*. According to tradition, the great Pisan scientist discovered the law of the pendulum by watching it swing back and forth.

Galileo's lamp, right; *Christ Enthroned between the Virgin and St. John the Evangelist,* detail of the mosaic in the bowl-shaped vault of the apse.
Opposite page: *the interior of the cathedral.*

THE PULPIT BY GIOVANNI PISANO

The most imposing monument in the cathedral is the pulpit sculpted by Giovanni Pisano in 1302-03; it was rebuilt in 1926 at the head of the main nave, to the left, after the dispersal caused by the fire. Before 1595 it was situated on the opposite side of the nave between the column and the supporting pillar of the dome, at the corner of the present choir stall. Pisano's pulpit, among all those produced by the second Pisan school, is certainly the richest, not only because of the nine reliefs of which it is composed, but also because of the supports of single or grouped figures and the various other sculpted sections. Next to the stupendous *Scenes from the Life of Christ* such as the moving, human scene of the *Nativity*, there are the crowds disturbed by violent motion that is ceaselessly transmitted from person to person, from group to group. This is done with such coherence that even inanimate objects participate and is reinforced by a dry, concise almost abbreviated form, which, however, is continuously adapted to expressing emotions. Pisano's sculpture becomes quite overpowering especially in the last five panels of the *Slaughter of the Innocents, Christ's Passion*, the *Crucifixion* and the *Last Judgement,* which is divided into two sections. In the Slaughter of the Innocents note Herod's imperious, michelangelesque gesture, the unleashed fury of the soldiers, and the mothers, resisting them with desperate cries.

Pulpit by *Giovanni Pisano*; below left: *detail of the panel of the Nativity;* right: *detail of the panel of the Crucifixion.*

THE LEANING TOWER

The most remarkable aspect of this tower - which sometimes overshadows its outstanding artistic merits - is, of course, the miracle of statics by which it has remained standing for centuries despite the fact that it leans sharply to the south. The tower was begun by Bonano Pisano in 1173 and had reached a height of some thirty-five feet when the ground unexpectedly subsided causing the first inclination of about 6 inches. The builder tried to correct the tilt from above, but reached the fourth floor without success. Work was therefore interrupted and was not resumed until 1234 when Wilhelm of Innsbruck built the tower up to the seventh floor. The full structure was realized by Tommaso Pisano when he added the bell chamber in 1350. The tower is 55.2 meters high (about 180 ft.) on the northern side, but only 54.5 meters high on the southern side. The inclination tends to increase by about one millimeter every year. Galileo Galilei carried out extensive studies on falling bodies from the top of the Leaning Tower. The tower is perfectly cylindrical in form and is designed in the Pisan Romanesque style. The entrance doorway leading inside is at the base. The doorway is adorned by a lunette with a sculpture depicting the *Virgin and Child between St. Peter and St. John the Baptist,* by Andrea Guardi, a member of the 14th century Pisan school. The interior has a spiral staircase of 294 steps leading to the top. At each floor there is a doorway which makes it possible to walk around the gallery on the outside, but since there are no safety railings this requires great care. There is a magnificent view of Pisa from the terrace above the top floor.

This page and next: *view of the Leaning Tower.*

THE BAPTISTRY

The Baptistry, begun in August 1152 when Pisa was at the height of its power underwent various vicissitudes during its construction. For a long time work was even suspended. Because of this, with the passing years, and changes in taste, considerable modifications were made, especially to its exterior. In all probability Diotisalvi carried out his original plan (which was supposed to have included a second gallery above the one that was built and a pyramid-shaped roof visible from the outside, like the church of Santo Sepolcro that he designed as well), up to a certain height that it is now difficult to establish. However, it is certain that the Romanesque structure was not substantially altered by the Gothic decoration superimposed on the original design. The ground floor is clearly Lombard in character with its four highly decorated and very deep portals, rare in Tuscany and especially around Pisa, and its arched windows which, like great splashes of shadow, lighten and decorate the broad arcades that support the loggia. The columns of the galleries each have a large dado on the capital which lends dynamic force to the arch. The arches, in turn, are decorated at the top and impost with human and animal heads and masks in the traditional Pisan-Romanesque style. The estimate of the time during which the decorative elements were added to Baptistry is based on these sculptures which, because of their fine quality, have been attributed to Nicola Pisano's circle and to his son, Giovanni. In fact, after a period of fervid work following the inception of the building when the internal ambulatory with its pillars and columns of granite from Elba and Sardinia were constructed, there was a long pause of about 50 years, towards the end of the 12th century. It was due more to a lack of money and possibly of some new ideas on how to continue building, rather than to the death of Diotisalvi. An inscription dated 1278 on a pilaster of the internal gallery states that building was resumed in that year. The Romanesque plan of the building prevails despite the sumptuous ornamentation of pinnacles, curls, spires and cusps, the lacy cornice that circles the Baptistry and bends at an acute angle over the round arches of the graceful double-lighted windows; and a tabernacle which adapts to the curvature of the cupola. When compared to the Gothic decoration (which does not correspond with the axis of the doorway and is not in harmony with the great windows, changing from cylindrical to polygonal near the cupola's base where the ribbing has nothing to do with the angles of the polygon), the prominent horizontal black stripes on the marble facing and overhanging middle cornice are an indication of the how such superficial additions do not in any way alter the structure of the Baptistry. Even the hemispheric cupola is a major departure from Diotisalvi's original design. While it amplifies and crowns the great mass, it is technically unnecessary from a static point of view. The dome is divided by scroll-motif marble mouldings. The five sections which face southeast have exposed lead sheeting, while the other half is covered in terra-cotta tile which contrasts strongly with the white marble.

Facing the cathedral, the portal with a highly accentu-

The Baptistry.

Detail of the loggia of the Baptistry,
decorated by *Nicola Pisano.*

ated splayed jamb is the most lavishly decorated, especially the archivolts that are concentrically divided with flowers and figures carved by various artists who lived in Pisa during the 12th century. Like the doors of other Pisan monuments, the classical influence is evident in the doorway's rectangular architrave. The two outermost columns, entirely carved with raceme plants, are reminiscent of the acanthus intaglio of the Ara Pacis Augustae and are interpreted with Romanesque strength. Certain details, uncommon for the 12th century, anticipate Renaissance motifs, such as the girls gathering fruit into a basket, watering flowers or playing the lyre.

Pulpit by *Nicola Pisano;* below, right: *Presentation in the Temple,*
detail of a panel on the pulpit by *Nicola Pisano.*

THE PULPIT BY NICOLA PISANO

The famous hexagonal pulpit carved by Nicola Pisano in 1260 bears a single inscription, the name of the great artist with whom the Romanesque period ended and the Gothic began. However, we must also remember the names of his helpers, especially Arnolfo, Fra Guglielmo and his son Giovanni, who along with their master, established the great school which in the 13th and then 14th century, with Andrea Pisano, Nino, Tommaso and Givoanni Balduccio, spread the influence of a style whose name and origins are Pisan. Nicola's pulpit, which breaks with tradition even in its hexagonal shape, is free standing and in close harmony with the architecture of the Baptistry and font. It at once summarizes the old, comprehends the present and interprets the future. Nicola was not insensitive to classical art which he studied at great length, to the extent of including figures he had seen in ancient Greek and Roman or Hellenistic bas-reliefs on the pulpit and other works such as the tomb of St. Dominic in Bologna.

THE MONUMENTAL CEMETERY

The Monumental Cemetery encloses the Piazza on the north with a long marble wall with blind arches, set on a high base. It is called "camposanto" (holy ground) because it contains earth taken from Mount Calvary in Palestine and brought to Pisa by the Archbishop Lanfranchi on his return from the crusades around 1200. It was his intention to consecrate the burial place of Pisans with earth sanctified by the presence of Christ. The work was begun in 1277 by Giovanni di Simone and completed, after many interruptions, during the second half of the 15th century. Conceived as an immense rectangular cloister, it communicates with the open space of the interior by means of six arches and large, round-arched windows. The latter were reduced in height in the 15th century and transformed into slim, four-lighted windows with delicate columns and pilasters supporting elaborate, intertwined cornice decorations in the Gothic style.

The Monumental Cemetery; above, left: ***The Tabernacle;*** inside, ***Virgin Enthroned with Saints and a Kneeling Figure,*** attributed to a *follower of Giovanni Pisano* (second half of the XIV century); below: ***the inside courtyard with the dome of the Del Pozzo Chapel.***

THE TRIUMPH OF DEATH

On the walls of the grand Salone del Camposanto is the great fresco cycle which includes the *Triumph of Death*, the *Last Judgement*, the *Inferno* and *Stories of the Anchorites* that have been attributed to Francesco Traini or Buffalmaco (mid 14th century). The Triumph of Death dominates the other frescoes through the clear unity of its grandiose compositions and its account of the human condition. In the center it shows Death's torment inflicted on humanity without respect or distinction for rank. Death, personified by a scrawny, ragged old woman, whip in hand, is preparing to strike a group of cheerful revelers in a flowering garden, ignoring the poor and unfortunate who are begging to be released from their suffering. On the left, a magnificent cavalcade of men and women finds itself facing three open coffins in which they see three dead bodies in an advanced state of decomposition. In front, a hermit (St. Macarius) reminds the riders, filled with horror and curiosity at this macabre spectacle, of the fleeting nature of life, the end that awaits all creatures and the need to prepare for death with a life dedicated to good works, far from evil, as chosen by the monks, intent on meditation and work (shown here and there in the upper left part of the fresco). The three coffins before which the riders have paused, covering their noses against the fetid smell of the bodies, illustrate the legend according to which the earth of the Camposanto possessed magical properties that enabled it to reduce the dead to skeletons within twenty four hours.

Above: *detail of the Last Judgement*; below: *the Cavalcade*, detail of the *Triumph of Death.*

THE MUSEUM OF THE SINOPIAS

The Museum of the Sinopias is currently housed in a wing of the former Ospedale della Misericordia that was built between 1257 and 1286 to plans by Giovanni di Simone.

The museum was opened in 1979, and it was destined to house and conserve the sinopias from the Monumental Cemetery. Sinopias are the preparatory drawings for frescoes, done directly on the walls. They were uncovered due to a tragic incident during World War II when a bomb exploded on the Camposanto, causing a devastating fire that destroyed most of the frescoes and left the few that remained in such terrible condition that they had to be removed for restoration. Thus, when the frescoes were taken off, the

preliminary drawings were brought to light, and were fixed onto special slabs and taken to a museum.

The museum is built on two levels. On the upper level are the panels with the oldest and most interesting sinopias such as the *Scenes from the Lives of the Holy Fathers,* the *Last Judgement,* the *Inferno* and the famous *Triumph of Death* all done by the hand of a great, unknown artist. In fact, he was known only as the Master of the Triumph of Death, and his identity was discovered by the art critic Luciano Bellosi in the 'fifties: Buonamico Buffalmaco.

On the ground floor are the sinopias by Benozzo Gozzoli which are entirely different in meaning and nature from those on the upper level. These are sketches, filled with references to daily life, and seem to plunge the viewer into the atmosphere of the times.

An interesting collection of water-colored drawings by Giampaolo Lasinio concludes the visit. These pictures give a clear and precise idea of European wall paintings in the 14th and 15th centuries.

Above, left: *the entrance to the Museum of the Sinopias*; center: *Annunciation* (detail), by *Benozzo Gozzoli*; below: *the ground floor of the museum.*

The portico of the Opera dell'Duomo with busts from the exterior loggia of the Baptistry;
below: ***headless statue of a woman,*** by *Giovanni Pisano* (XIV century).

MUSEO DELL'OPERA DEL DUOMO

The building that houses the Museo dell'Opera del Duomo stands on the south east corner of the grassy, lonely Piazza dei Miracoli. The view from the upper loggia that runs along the old cloister is truly spectacular. It triggers a sequence of subtle references and meanings, and creates a marvelous link between the works of art in the museum and the monuments to which they originally belonged. The building, initially constructed to house the Cathedral Canons (who lived there from around 1100 to the early 17th century) was later destined for other uses. Its current configuration dates from the early 17th century when it was completely rebuilt to house the Diocesan Seminary. Later it became private proper-

ty and in 1784 it was the headquarters of the academy of fine arts, home of Giovanni Rosini (man of letters), until 1887 when the Capuchin sisters moved in and transformed the complex into a cloistered convent. In 1979 it was purchased by the Opera della Primaziale in order to establish a true Museo dell'-Opera. The museum was opened in 1986. Through its treasures and many works of art it tells the long and complicated story of the Pisan primacy, its famous monuments and the city's cultural and artistic history.

The oldest and most famous core of the collection is located on the ground floor and in the portico. This comprises sculptures from the 12th to 17th centuries, including masterpieces by Nicola and Giovanni Pisano, Tino di Camaino and Nino Pisano. One room and the adjacent chapel contain the **Cathedral Treasure.** This is a collection of precious liturgical items and

Above, from the left: *The Virgin of the Conversation* by *Giovanni Pisano* (c. 1280); *the Gryphon* (XII century); below, left: *the Ivory Madonna* by *Giovanni Pisano* (late XII century); right: *the wooden Christ from the cathedral* (latter half of the XII century).

objects from the Medieval cathedral, including the famous ivory Madonna by Giovanni Pisano and silverware made from the 16th to the 19th centuries. The displays are presented chronologically and informatively. On the first floor there are sculptures and paintings from the 16th to the 19th centuries, monumental wooden inlays, illuminated Medieval choir-books, paraments, liturgical clothing and textiles, a collection of Egyptian, Etruscan and Roman items and finally a group of graphics with the famous nineteenth century engravings by Carlo Lasinio, first conservator of the Monumental Cemetery.

Palazzo dei Cavalieri or della Carovana; below: *the coat of arms of the Knights of St. Stephen.*

PIAZZA DEI CAVALIERI

This was once the site of the Roman forum; during the Middle Ages it became the city's political center where the Pisans used to hold democratic meetings to discuss issues concerning the life of the free city-state. The Republic's triumphs and victories were celebrated in this square, and it was here that the Commissariat of the Republic announced the end of Pisan independence in 1406. Today, the square retains its Renaissance appearance, for which Giorgio Vasari, commissioned by the Medici, is responsible. In 1561 Cosimo I dei Medici, Grand Duke of Tuscany (his 14th century statue stands in the Piazza) founded the religious-military order of the Knights of St. Stephen on whose behalf the church of the Cavalieri was built between 1565 and 1569. The plans were drawn by Giorgio Vasari, but other Florentine architects also worked with the great master. It is the only Renaissance church in a city where the Romanesque reigns unchallenged. The building that stands near the church of the Cavalieri was renovated by Giorgio Vasari, who also did the decorations on the façade along with his pupils. The building, which was originally the knights' military training quarters, now houses the Scuola Normale Superiore, an institute of higher education founded by Napoleon in 1810.

PALAZZO DELLA GHERARDESCA

The Palazzo dell'Orologio, now known as Palazzo della Gherardesca was also built for the Knights of St. Stephen in 1607 to plans by Vasari. Count Ugolino, mentioned by Dante in a famous canto of The Inferno, was imprisoned in the Gualandi tower and left to die with his children and grandchildren.

Right: *Palazzo della Gherardesca*; below: *a Grand Duke of Tuscany,* the bust is an oval niche on the façade of the Palazzo dei Cavalieri.

PALAZZO DEI CAVALIERI

This building was once known as Palazzo della Carovana (of the caravan), since it was here that the Knights attended an initiation course called "caravan" (from the Persian word for company or journey). In the Middle Ages it was the Palazzo degli Anziani del Popolo (a government building), and like the church was remodeled by Vasari in 1562. The lovely graffito decorations on the façade, restored at the beginning of the 20th century, are original. The façade has a double staircase, and the niches between the third and fourth stories contain busts of the Medici Grand Dukes.

The facade of the Palazzo dei Cavalieri.

SANTO STEFANO DEI CAVALIERI

This great church was built by Vasari in 1569. The façade, of a later date, is by Giovanni de'Medici. It is flanked by two low buildings despoiled by the Cavalieri and transformed into naves during the 17th century. War trophies of the Order, notably Turkish flags, hang on the inside walls. The beautiful ceiling is of carved wood, Behind the great Baroque high altar (a 17th century work by Francesco Silvani and Giovanni Battista Foggini) is a gilded bronze reliquary bust of *San Rossore* by Donatello (1427).

The façade of Santo Stefano dei Cavalieri.

SANTA MARIA DELLA SPINA

This tiny building, erected in 1323, is a jewel of Pisan Gothic architecture. Its name derives from a reliquary containing a thorn ("spina") supposedly from Christ's crown of thorns. The building originally stood on the river bank, but constantly threatened by floods and dampness, it was dismantled in 1870 and rebuilt on a safer spot at street level. The exterior of the marble-faced church is elaborately decorated, especially the side facing the Arno. The 13 tabernacles on the upper section of the building are filled with statues of *Christ* and the 12 *Apostles* attributed to followers of Giovanni Pisano. The whole building is crowned with intricately carved spires and pinnacles as well as figures of *saints* and *angels*. The façade is adorned with two rose-windows and three cusps. In the tabernacle in the middle are statues of the *Virgin and Child and Two Angels*. The altar inside is decorated with sculptures by Tommaso Pisano.

Above: *the façade of Santa Maria della Spina*; below, left: *the church seen from the Lungarno*; right: *detail of the interior.*

Left: *the façade of the church of San Paolo a Ripa d'Arno;* right: *the octagonal chapel of Sant'Agata;* below: *details of the decorations above the main portal of the church of San Paolo.*

SAN PAOLO A RIPA D'ARNO

This superb example of Pisan Romanesque architecture was actually founded in the 9th century. Over the centuries it has been remodeled several times (the most recent restoration dates from 1943). The typically Pisan façade, with a lower section of arches topped by three rows of loggias, is faced in striped marble. Inside, the three naves are separated by granite columns with their splendid original capitals. Above the presbytery is a huge dome. On the right is the *tomb of Burgundio* made from a Roman sarcophagus. In the left nave is a painting of the *Virgin and Child with Saints* dated 1397, by Turino Vanni. A lovely 14th century stained glass window illuminates the apse. Behind the church, in the middle of a lawn, is the tiny **Chapel of Sant'Agata**, built in the 12th century and attributed to Diotisalvi. The sole decorative motifs on the plain, octagonal brick building are the three-lighted windows and the cusp.

The church of San Matteo and the adjacent entrance to the National Museum.

THE MUSEO NAZIONALE DI SAN MATTEO

The museum occupies thirty-eight rooms of a former Benedictine monastery that was restored and

Above, from the left: *the Madonna del Latte,* attributed to *Nino Pisano;* **Madonna and Child with Saints** (detail), polyptych by *Simone Martini;* below, from the left: **St. Paul** by *Masaccio;* **Crucifix** by *Giunta Pisano.*

remodeled in 1949. The collection was started in the 18th century by Mons. Zucchetti and donated to the Opera del Duomo in 1796. Over the years, works from suppressed monasteries and convents and private bequests contributed to the collection's growth. Today, the exhibits provide an excellent and chronological introduction to and understanding of how art developed in Pisa. The splendid masterpieces by Giovanni Pisano and Andrea Pisano alone would make the museum famous. Of particular note are the works of the Pisan Primitive school; Giunta Pisano and the great, unknown Master of San Martino are

Above, from the left: *St. Sebastian and St. Rocco* by *Domenico Ghirlandaio*; *Madonna and Child* by *Gentile da Fabriano*; below, from the left: *Crucifix* by *Berlinghieri*; *Madonna and Child with Scenes from Her Life*, by the *Maestro di San Martino*.

represented by exceptional paintings. As can be seen here, these early Pisans were undoubtedly the precursors of Cimabue and Duccio di Buoninsenga. Simone Martini painted the extraordinary *polyptych* in 1313 for the church of Santa Caterina. This masterpiece definitely ranks among the finest works of 14th century Italian painting. An extraordinarily delicate sculptural masterpiece is the Madonna del Latte, attributed to Nino Pisano. There is also an interesting group of tapestries and illuminated manuscripts.

FOLKLORE

THE ST. RANIERI BOAT RACE

The race is held on June 17, the feast of St. Ranieri, with the various districts of the city as participants. After having sailed approximately one mile to the finish line, a member of the crew of each boat must climb a pole and take down a flag. The winners get a cup, the losers...a pair of ducks.

THE BOAT RACE OF THE MARITIME REPUBLICS

This historic regatta was first raced in 1956 and the idea, which originated in Pisa, has turned out to be a big national and international success. Once every four years, Pisa, Amalfi, Genoa and Venice play host to the race which is an attempt to perpetuate the memory and splendor of the old maritime republics. Before the race there is a fantastic parade in historic dress. The figurehead of each boat is the symbol of its republic: the eagle for Pisa, the winged horse for Amalfi, the winged dragon for Genoa and the Lion of St. Mark for Venice.

THE GIOCO DEL PONTE

This sham battle was originally called the Gioco del Mazzascudo and used to be held in Piazza dei Cavalieri. It served mainly to keep Pisan youths trained in the arts of war. Later the game was played on the "Ponte di Mezzo". Since the Arno River divides Pisa into two parts, the southern side was called "*Mezzogiorno*" and the northern side "*Tramontana*". Knights and soldiers dressed in armor and carrying special shields called "tartoni" fight to capture the bridge.

SIENA

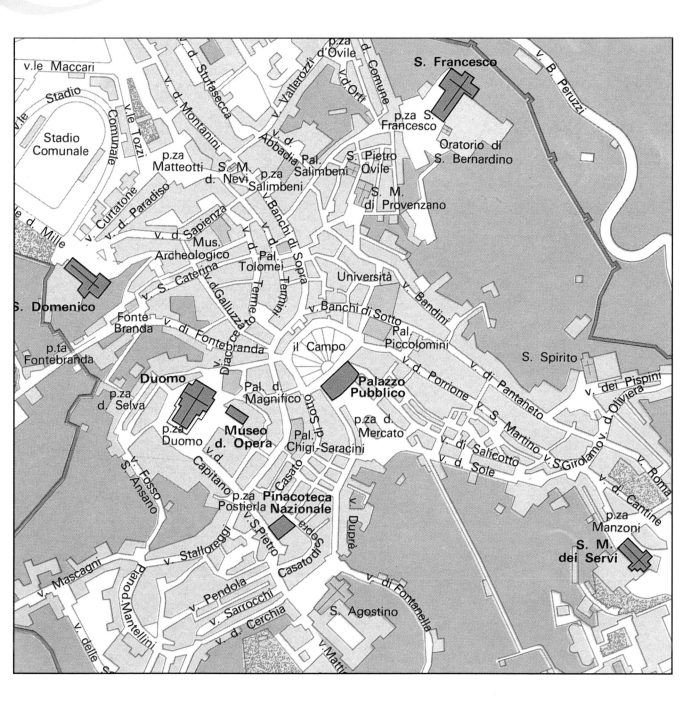

According to an old legend Siena was founded by Aschius and Senius, the sons of Remus (the brother of Romulus , the mythical founder of Rome), spreading over the three hills that it still occupies today. Another legend attributes its founding to the Senonic Gauls. In any case, it was certainly a subject of Rome in the Imperial era, with the name of Sena Julia. In 1147 the city, which already had a flourishing trade, shook off the feudal yoke and became a free city-state. This was the beginning of its most splendid, and at the same time, most tormented period, torn by internal power struggles. Moreover, on the external front, there was continuous and bitter rivalry with Guelph Florence with which Ghibelline Siena was often at war, meeting with varying fortunes. Nonetheless, the great families of Sienese bankers and merchants thrived and did good business with the whole of Europe. A pause took place in the second half of the 13th century. Siena defeated Florence at Montaperti in 1260 and obtained a momentary Ghibelline supremacy in Tuscany. However, this provoked a reaction on the part of the Papacy which stopped its dealings with the Sienese banks and excommunicated the city. The Sienese, worried about their economy, were "converted" (with a few exceptions) to the Guelph cause. Trade flourished once more and peace reigned in Tuscany until the plague and famine during the middle of the 14th century caused fresh instability and economic difficulties. At the end of the century the city was ruled by the Visconti, and then Pandolfo Petrucci. In 1555, after a long siege Siena was conquered by Florence. Apart from wars and economic development, the Middle Ages were a period of prolific and flourishing artistic production. The elegant, refined painting of Duccio di Buoninsenga, Simone Martini and Lorenzetti allowed Siena to contend with Florence for supremacy in Italian Gothic art. Today Siena is a city of art and culture that preserves its old appearance: its splendid monuments make it one of the most beautiful cities in Italy.

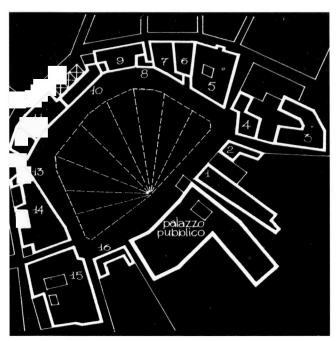

Map of Piazza del Campo.

1. Palazzo Petroni
2. Palazzo Piccolomini Salamoneschi
3. Palazzo Piccolomini
4. Palazzo Ragnoni
5. Palazzo Mezolombardi-Rinaldini
6. Palazzo Tornainpuglia Sansedoni
7. Palazzo Vincenti
8. Palazzo Piccolomini
9. Palazzo Rimbotti
10. Palazzo della Mercanzia
11. Palazzo Saracini
12. Palazzo Scotti
13. Palazzo Accarigi
14. Palazzo Alessi
15. Palazzo Mattasala Lambertini
16. Casa Beringeri-Antolini

PIAZZA DEL CAMPO

This, the largest piazza in Siena is formed by the junction of the three hills over which the city extends meeting in a plateau that has become the great piazza, known as the "campo" (field) to recall its original rustic appearance. The present arrangement of the piazza dates back to the 12th and 13th century. The piazza slopes down towards the Palazzo Pubblico and is paved with bricks, and divided into nine segments separated by strips of stone. Ancient palaces surround the piazza. Next to Via Rinaldini is **Palazzo Chigi-Zondadari**, built at a very early period, but restored to its present form by Antonio Valeri in 1724. **Palazzo Sansedoni**, with its fine curving red brick façade, stands immediately next to it. Continuing between the alleyways of San Pietro and San Paolo, is the back of the **Loggia della Mercanzia** built to plans by Ferdinando Fuga in 1763; next to it are the ancient Gothic **De Metz houses**, and after Costarella dei Barbieri, the crenellated 16th century **Palazzo d'Elci**.

Aerial view of the Piazza del Campo.

THE PALIO

For most Italian and foreign tourists the Palio is a colorful festival, with a spectacular historic parade, and the thrills of watching fearless jockeys. For the Sienese, however, it goes beyond mere entertainment. For them the Palio is a symbol of liberty, of the power and grandeur of the Sienese Republic. This explains the rivalry between the various Contradas and the incredible passion that pervades all Sienese during the preparation and actual running of the Palio. The two important dates (2 July and 16 August) revive fine memories every year, along with the rivalries and disagreements that are centuries old. Each Contrada becomes a small country to defend and lead to victory. The Palio delle Contrade as we know it today was created in the 17th century, even though the race is much older. It seems that in the past Siena had fifty nine Contradas. Today there are only seventeen, ten of which, either by turn, or by drawings, participate in this wonderful race under their own banners: *Aquila, Chiocciola, Onda, Pantera, Selva, Tartuca, Civetta, Leocorno, Nicchio, Torre, Valdimontone, Bruco, Drago, Giraffa, Istrice, Lupa* and *Oca*. The jockeys dressed the colors of their Contrada, with helmets, ride out of the courtyard of the Palazzo Comunale. Each rides bareback and it is easy to imagine what a difficult time they have to remain mounted. As they leave the palace the jockeys are given whips to use on their horses, but they also use them on their rivals and their respective horses. The horses line up for the start in front of the judges' box, when the starting tape is lowered they take off to run around the piazza three times. Jockeys often fall; in these cases if the horse reaches the finish line first, even without a rider, it still wins the race. The winner (the jockey) is carried triumphantly through the streets by his fellows from the Contrada, and the winning Contrada celebrates its victory with a great outdoor dinner...the horse also participates.

The old Gaia fountain in a nineteenth century photo;
below: *detail of Palazzo Sansedoni.*

THE GAIA FOUNTAIN

I n the center of the magnificent fan-shaped piazza is the monumental Gaia fountain which was encased with marble and statuary between 1409 and 1419 by the famous Sienese sculptor Jacopo della Quercia. The fountain was called "Gaia" after the celebrations that were held for the completion of the work. The very fine bas-reliefs suffered the wear and tear of time and in 1868 were replaced with free versions by the sculptor Tito Sarrocchi (the originals are kept in the Palazzo Pubblico). The fountain, supplied with water by a 14th century aqueduct 15 miles long, is on a square plan and has a marble parapet with niches and columns on three sides. The niches contain representations of the *Theological Virtues* and two scenes from *Genesis*, the *Creation of Adam and Eve* and the *Expulsion of Adam and Eve from the Garden of Eden*.

THE SANSEDONI PALACE

T he façade is a lively red, with three tiers of three-lighted windows, while on the left stands the fine tower that repeats the same ornamental motifs (it was once so high that it competed for supremacy with the tower of Palazzo Pubblico). Built in 1216, Palazzo Sansedoni did not at first have its present magnificent appearance which is the result of rebuilding carried out by Agostino di Giovanni in 1339. Inside the palace is a chapel dedicated to the Dominican friar, the Blessed Ambrogio Sansedoni, which, according to tradition was his bedroom. This was built in 1692 and the vault is frescoed by Antonio Domenico Gabbioni. On the altar is a bas-relief representing the *Virgin appearing to the Blessed Ambrogio Sansedoni* by Giuseppe Mazzuoli, and on the walls are fine, bronze bas-reliefs by Soldani.

THE TORRE DEL MANGIA

On one side of the palace soars the elegant, high brick shaft of the Mangia Tower, below which is the Piazza Chapel. The tower's curious name derives from a popular nickname for the bellringer, Giovanni or Bartolomeo di Duccio who was known as Mangiaguadagni ("eat your earnings") or Mangia (simply "eat"). His place was taken by a wooden robot, constructed by Dello Delli in 1426. This was rebuilt in copper and then in stone, and inherited the first bell-ringer's name becoming as popular in Siena as "Pasquino" in Rome, until it was removed in 1780. The tower is over 102 yards high and was built by Minuccio and Francesco di Rinaldo between 1338 and 1348. Over the bell chamber, built of white stone by Agostino di Giovanni to plans by Lippo Memmi, hangs an enormous bell weighing over six tons (1666).

The Torre del Mangia; below: the Piazza Chapel.

THE PIAZZA CHAPEL

In the form of a loggia at the foot of the tower, this chapel was built between 1352 and 1376 in honor of the Virgin Mary who freed the city from the scourge of the plague (1348). The chapel was begun to plans by Domenico di Agostino and rebuilt several times, receiving its final form from Giovanni di Cecco. The lower part is early, but the upper part was built in Renaissance style by Antonio Federighi in 1463-68, with arches and the crowning part. The niches in the pillars contain statues of saints made between 1377 and 1381. The fifteenth century wrought iron gate is by Conte di Lelio Orlandi. On the altar is a restored fresco by Sodoma with *Madonna, Saints and the Eternal Father* (1539).

From the left: *the courtyard of the Palazzo del Comune* and *the Palazzo del Comune*; below: *detail of a view of Siena* in a painting by *Sano di Pietro* (Pinacoteca Nazionale).

THE PALAZZO PUBBLICO

The magnificent and imposing palace dominates Piazza del Campo. It was the seat of the Government of the Republic, then of the Podestà and at present houses the Municipal Government. The wonderful, curved Gothic building was originally composed only of the central part which had three stories and was practically a tower house. The building was probably designed by the architects Agostino di Giovanni and Agnolo di Ventura. It was built between 1279 and 1310 in stone on the ground floor and above this in red brick. In 1327 it was enlarged on the right side with the addition of the prisons, and in 1342 the Great Council Hall. In the 17th century the two side wings were raised one story. In the center of the palace at the top is the great disc with the *Monogram of Christ* (the emblem of St. Bernardino), painted in 1425 by Battista di Niccolò da Padova, while the rays and copper decoration are by Turino di Sano and his son Giovanni. The great Medici coat of arms in the middle of the façade, above the first row of windows, was placed there in 1560. Beside it are two other coats of arms: on the right the *Florentine Lion Rampant* and on the left, the *Sienese shield* or *balzana* whose colors, black and white are repeated in the ogival tympanum of the elegant three-lighted windows and those on the ground floor. At the corner of the right side of the palace is a column with a Corinthian capital which bears the copy of another Sienese emblem, the *she-wolf suckling the twins*. The original in gilded tin by Giovanni and Lorenzo Turino, 1429-30, is inside the palace in the entrance hall of the Civic Museum. The doorway, on the right of the Piazza Chapel leads into the massive 14th century brick **courtyard of the Podestà**, with its powerful octagonal pillars and wide arches. Looking up from here there is a magnificent view of the Mangia Tower. On the walls of the courtyard are various coats of arms of the rulers of the Republic; on the left the remains of a 14th century fresco of the *Madonna and Saints*, and below, the *mutilated statue of Mangia*. Opposite this is the entrance to the **Teatro Rinnovati** which was built inside the former Great Council Hall by Riccio in 1560: twice damaged by fire, the theater was rebuilt in 1753 and restored in 1951.

THE MAP ROOM

This room takes its name from a lost work, painted by Ambrogio Lorenzetti depicting a globe. On the left, at the end of the room is the splendid fresco of the *Maestà* by Simone Martini, of the *Madonna Enthroned with the Child with two angels at the sides.* She is surrounded by the *patron saints of Siena*: *Ansano, Vittore, Crescenzio* and *Savino*; all around are 32 figures of *Apostles, Saints, Doctors* and *Prophets*. This painting was the first work by Simone; it was executed four years after the famous Maestà which Duccio di Buoninsenga, Simone's master, painted for the cathedral and which is now in the Museo dell'Opera del Duomo. A comparison between the two works is of great interest. The pupil, while not forgetting the orig-

inal manner of Duccio who liked to dwell on the delicate profiles of angels and saints, speaks a new language and has a strong feeling for line. For Simone line is everything, flowing with surprising facility, creating forms that are clothed with an exquisite enamelled color. The suffused luminosity of the gilding, the freshness of the color, the surprising expressive intensity of the faces, make this first work a significant example of the revival in Sienese painting. On the opposite wall, above, is another masterpiece by Simone Martini, *Guidoriccio da Fogliano at the siege of the Castle of Montemassi*, painted in 1328 (recently, doubts have been cast as to the attribution of this work to Simone). The fresco may be usefully compared to the contemporary paintings by Giotto who prefers the figure in his compositions, giving it more importance than the setting. With Simone, the opposite happens: he is principally sensitive to the environment to which the figure is subordinated. There is a symbolic subject here: the condottiere makes his triumphant way through a fabulous landscape scattered with castles he has conquered. Below the fresco on the left, *Sant'Ansano baptizing* and

Above: *Guidoriccio da Fogliano at the siege of the Castle of Montemassi* (detail), by *Simone Martini;* below: *the Map Room.*

"Maestà"; below: *Guidoriccio da Fogliano at the siege of the Castle of Montemassi,* two works by *Simone Martini.*

on the right *San Vittore*, two fine monumental figures frescoed by Sodoma in 1529. In the middle, there are the remains of another 14th century fresco of unknown attribution which clearly shows the marks left by the rotating globe. On the wall with the window is a large *monogram of St. Bernardino*; on the wall with the arches, above right, the *Victory of the Sienese over the Florentines at Poggio Imperiale near Poggibonsi on September 8, 1479*, a fresco by Giovanni di Cristofano and Francesco d'Andrea (1480); on the left, the *Victory of the Sienese over the English Company of the Hat at Sinalunga in 1363*, a fresco attributed to Lippo Vanni or Luca di Tommé (1370). On the pillars, (starting from the right) are the *Blessed Andrea Gallerani* and the *Blessed Ambrogio Sansedoni*, executed in the 16th century by followers Riccio's school.

Allegory of Good Government by *Ambrogio Lorenzetti*; below: ***detail of the Allegory of Peace and of Good Government*** by *Ambrogio Lorenzetti.*

THE ROOM OF PEACE

This was the room used for the meetings of the Lords or Government of Nine, to whom the fine frescoes by Ambrogio Lorenzetti, executed between 1338 and 1340, are dedicated. The paintings illustrate the *Effects of Good Government in the town and country* and those of *Bad Government*. The whole composition covers three walls, The central one has the *allegory of Good Government*; on the right wall are the *Effects of Good Government* and on the one opposite the *Effects of Bad Government*. Good Government is symbolized by the austere old King dressed in the black and white colors of the Sienese shield. He is surrounded by the *Civic Virtues* on the right, *Magnanimity, Temperance* and *Justice*, and on the left, *Prudence, Strength* and *Peace*. Above the king are the *theological virtues* of *Faith, Hope* and *Charity*, and at his feet, the wolf suckling the twins; beside him, on the right, is a victorious Sienese army with its prisoners; on the left side, Justice looking at Wisdom who holds the scales helped by two angels. All this allegory of Good and Bad Government follows a precise moral and political aim and is both an exaltation of the programmatic and ideal wisdom of the government by the party of Nine and a highly significant representation of the life and customs of society at that time, not only in Siena, but all over Italy. On the right wall is the *Effects of Good Government*, in the town and country which gives us an illustration of town and of country life. On the left wall, the *allegory of the Effects of Bad Government*. This is in poor condition, but the essence can still be made out. On the right is the terrible horned figure of *Tyranny* surrounded by *Cruelty, Deceit, Fraud, Fury, Discord* and *Perfidy*; below, *Humiliated Justice*; above, *Greed, Pride* and *Vanity*. The rest of the composition represents the effects of Bad Government with illustrations of devastation, murder, theft and an abandoned countryside.

THE CATHEDRAL

A cathedral existed on the site of the present one ever since the 9th century. In 1196 the Opera di Santa Maria was constituted by the Bishop and the city-state. This new organization was to superintend the rebuilding of the church. The main part of the building, both inside and outside, was completed between 1259 and 1264. In 1317 it was decided to enlarge the cathedral. Camaino di Crescentino was appointed to design the building, but his solution did not meet with approval, and it was agreed to build a new cathedral in such a way that the existing one would become the transept. This grandiose and ambi-tious plan reflected the prosperity and spiritual exalta-tion of the people of Siena. Work was started in 1339. However this fine dream could not be realized for political reasons, and mainly because of the plague in 1348 which put a stop to work and made it necessary to go back to the original plan by Camaino di Cres-centino. The subject of the decorations on the façade is the *Glorification of the Virgin Mary*, protectress of Siena. As can be seen, it is in two different styles. The lower part is Romanesque with Gothic influences, the upper is decorated Italian Gothic. The Romanesque part and the three portals are by Giovanni Pisano and pupils including Tino di Camaino. They worked on it between 1284 and 1333.

Below: *apsidal view of the Cathedral with the unfinished façade.*
Opposite page: *the façade of the cathedral.*

THE INTERIOR - The interior of the cathedral is shaped like a Latin cross with three wide naves divided by clustered, Romanesque pillars that show some Gothic influence. The floor is divided into 56 squares illustrating religious scenes, made by over 40 artists, including Pietro del Minella, Beccafumi and Pinturicchio, who worked on it from 1396 to 1547. The finest of these squares are covered with boards and are only on view to the public between August 15 and September 15 every year. On the first pillars are two very fine *holy water stoups* by Antonio Federighi (1463). At the beginning of the right nave is a *statue of Paul V* by Fulvio Signorini (1605). Further along, on the left, at the center of the transept, six pillars support the dome, the lower part of which is hexagonal and the upper dodecagonal. At the corners of the pillars there are statues of *Saints* and in the columned gallery above, 46 figures of *Patriarchs* and *Prophets*. At the opposite side of the crossing is the *pulpit* by Nicola Pisano. At the beginning of the right transept, on the right, is the **Chapel of Vows**, or **Chigi Chapel**, in the form of a temple, built by Alexander VII in the 17th century. The painting of the *Madonna and Child* on the altar has been attributed to Guido da Siena.

The *statues of St. Jerome, St. Mary Magdalene*, and the *Angels* as well as the altar are by Gian Lorenzo Bernini. The altar in the main chapel, by Peruzzi (1532) has a bronze ciborium by Vecchietta. The two *Angels* at the sides are by Giovanni di Stefano (1489) and the two lower down are by Francesco di Giorgio (1499). On the corbels of the pillars there are eight *Angels* by Beccafumi (1550). The apse has finely carved wooden choirstalls by Fra Giovanni da Verona (1503). Above the fine round glass window with *Scenes from the Life of the Virgin Mary* is a work from 1288 made to cartoons by Duccio. At the end of the right transept is the Renaissance **chapel of St. John the Baptist**, by Giovanni di Stefano (1482). It has a very fine doorway and contains excellent art works, including the bronze *statue of St. John the Baptist* by Donatello (1457) and the *statue of St. Catherine* by Neroccio (1487). The frescoes by Pinturicchio with *scenes from Life of St. John the Baptist* are exceptional as are the bas-reliefs of *Adam and Eve* on the baptismal font, by Federighi. In the fourth bay of the left nave is the magnificent *Piccolomini altar* by Andrea Bregno (1481-1485). The *Virgin and Child* is by Paolo Fei and the four very fine statues have been attributed to Michelangelo.

Below: *the Piccolomini Library*; right: *detail of the Epiphany* by *Pietro Sorri*.
Opposite page: *the central nave in the Cathedral.*

PICCOLOMINI LIBRARY

The entrance to the library is at the end of the left nave of the cathedral. It was founded in 1495 by Cardinal Francesco Piccolomini, later Pope Pius III, as a tribute to his uncle, Pope Pius II. The interior was frescoed by Pinturicchio with scenes from the Life of Pius II: *the departure of Piccolomini for the Council of Basel; Ambassador to the court of King James of Scotland; he is crowned poet by the Emperor Frederick III; he is sent by Frederick as ambassador to Pope Eugenius IV; he presents Eleonora of Portugal to Frederick III; he is created Cardinal by Callixtus III; he is elected Pope; he preaches in Mantua for the crusade against the Turks; he canonizes St. Catherine of Siena; he dies in Ancona.* In the middle of the room is the famous Roman sculpture of the *Three Graces* (3rd century A.D.).

Pulpit by *Nicola Pisano*; right: ***detail of the Redeemer.***

THE PULPIT BY NICOLA PISANO

The most important artwork in the cathedral is situated at the beginning of the left transept, near the hexagon of the dome. The great masterpiece of sculpture is the *pulpit* by Nicola Pisano who was assisted by his 20 year old son, Giovanni and his pupils, Arnolfo di Cambio, Donato di Ricevuto and Lapo Ciuccio di Ciuto (1265-68). Before the cathedral was enlarged on the side of the presbytery, the pulpit stood below the cupola, between the first two pillars, and its base of columns and lions rested on the brick floor. When the church was enlarged the pulpit was removed (1543) and placed where it is now, on a marble pedestal to make it more imposing; the original staircase was replaced by a gold one made to designs by Bartolomeo Neroni, called Riccio (1570). It is on an octagonal plan and rests on three-lobed arches at the corners of which are representations of the *Virtues*. It is supported by eight columns at the sides and one in the middle. Those at the sides stand on bases and on lions. The central one has an octagonal base that supports a sculpture group of eight figures portraying the *Seven Liberal Arts* and *Music*. The parapet, comprising seven panels divided by figures of *Angels* and *Prophets*, has bas-reliefs with scenes of the *Life of Christ*: the *Nativity* and the *Visitation,* the *Arrival* and *Adoration of the Magi*; the *Presentation in the Temple* and the *Flight into Egypt*; the *Slaughter of the Innocents*; the *Crucifixion* and *Symbols of the Evangelists*; the *Last Judgment of the Wicked*; the *Last Judgement of the Elect.* Nicola d'Apulia better known as Nicola Pisano had already sculpted the pulpit in the Baptistry in Pisa (1260), but reached the apex of his achievement as a sculptor here in Siena. He reveals his careful study of ancient art which he adapts to the new Gothic taste using a highly lyrical style of sculpture, and treating the narrative with a great sense of equilibrium. The greatest effect and dramatic intensity are achieved in the panels of the *Crucifixion* and the *Last Judgement*.

Opposite page, above: *Articles of the Credo with the Resurrection of Christ* by *Vecchietta;* below, from the left: *the façade and interior of the Bapitstry.*

THE BAPTISTRY

The Gothic façade is a masterpiece attributed, with some uncertainty, to Jacopo di Mino del Pelliciaio. It was built between 1317 and 1382, but the upper part was not completed. The architectural composition is admirable for its harmony and elegance, especially in the three doorways. The rectangular interior has three naves and a small apse.

The building was designed by Camaino di Crescentino and his son Tino di Camaino (1325). In the center there is a *marble font*, a marvelous creation by the sculptor Jacopo della Quercia (1417-30). The *Statue of St. John the Baptist* above the ciborium is also by Jacopo della Quercia. Of the four bronze *angels* at the corners between the pediments, three were done by the great Donatello and one by Giovanni di Turino (1424). In the niches there are five figures of *Prophets* by Jacopo della Quercia and a fine *Virgin and Child* by Giovanni di Turino. On the font itself there are six gilded bronze panels (separated by statues) illustrating the *Life of St. John the Baptist* by Jacopo della Quercia, Donatello, Lorenzo Ghiberti and others. The greatest Sienese and Florentine sculptors collaborated on this wonderful font, but the most expressive and dramatic work with its creative sense and feeling for perspective is by Donatello, especially in *Herod's Banquet*.

MUSEO DELL'OPERA DEL DUOMO

This museum was opened in 1870 to house works from the Cathedral and the Baptistry. On the first floor a special room contains the famous Maestà altar piece by Duccio di Buoninsegna. This splendid altarpiece, destined for the main altar in the Cathedral was made between 1308 and 1311. While it was being transferred from the artist's house to the cathedral there was great public rejoicing to celebrate the masterpiece. However, the work has not survived in its entirety. Painted on both sides with predellas and cusps, it was originally composed of 60 squares representing episodes in the *Life of Christ* and the *Virgin Mary*. Sixteen of the squares were on the side facing the congregation; there were also 7 figures of *prophets* and 10 busts of *apostles*. The entire work stood on the altar from 1311 to 1505. In 1771 the two sides were separated and placed in the Chapels of the Blessed Sacrament and of Sant'Ansano. Finally, in 1878 after other moves and manipulations, it found a permanent home in this museum. The title "Maestà" or Majesty is derived from the Medieval term for images of the Virgin enthroned with the Child. The work is still Byzantine in theme, but the entire composition of the Virgin seated on the throne with Angels and Saints is treated with a new grace, sensitivity and sweetness.

In the twenty-six squares on the rear side, which

Nativity of the Virgin, by *Pietro Lorenzetti.*

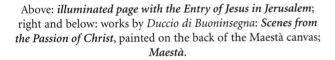

represent episodes from the *Life of Christ*, the artist achieves the height of stylistic perfection. The design shrewdly and gently expresses the psychology of the figures; the sumptuous colors create a special version of reality in which there is no dramatic tension or stress so that the various episodes have a calm, peaceful quality, a gentle melancholy that lends itself perfectly to the mystic ideal of the era. Among the many important works in the Museum the following items deserve special mention: the *Nativity of the Virgin*, a masterpiece by Pietro Lorenzetti signed and dated 1342; the 13th century gilt reliquary containing the *head of St. Galgano*; a *Madonna and Child*, early work by Duccio di Buoninsegna; sculptures by Giovanni Pisano and Jacopo della Quercia, and finally the *Blessed Agostino Novelli inspired by an Angel and Four of his Miracles*, a masterpiece by Simone Martini (c. 1330).

Above: *illuminated page with the Entry of Jesus in Jerusalem*; right and below: works by *Duccio di Buoninsegna*: *Scenes from the Passion of Christ*, painted on the back of the Maestà canvas; *Maestà*.

THE PINACOTECA NAZIONALE

This museum is located in the Palazzo Buonsignori-ni. It is one of the finest Gothic palaces in Siena made of brick with crenellations, a stone base and two rows of elegant, three-lighted windows by Cristoforo di Mone di Pasquino (1458). The gallery (Pinacoteca Nazionale) was established in its current headquarters in 1932, but was actually started in 1816 as the Gallery of the Provincial Institute of the Fine Arts. The main works include: the *Madonna of the Franciscans* a famous, delicate work by Duccio di Buoninsegna; a *Madonna and Child* by Simone Martini; *Madonna and child, Saints, Angels and Doctors of the Church* and an *Annunciation* by Ambrogio Lorenzetti. Two small paintings on wood, a *Castle on the shore of a Lake* and a *View of the City by the Sea*, the first examples of landscape painting in Medieval Italian art, have also been attributed to Ambrogio. There are also *Stories of Carmelites* by Pietro Lorenzetti, and other works by Pinturicchio, Dürer and Lotto.

On this page, two works by *A. Lorenzetti:* ***Annunciation of the Virgin*** and ***View of the City by the Sea*** (below).
Opposite page: ***Madonna of the Franciscans***, by *Duccio di Buoninsegna.*

SAN FRANCESCO

Built in 1326 over a small early church dedicated to St. Peter, the Gothic basilica was erected according to plans by Agostino d'Agnolo, but was completed in 1475 perhaps to drawings by Francesco di Giorgio. In 1655 it was damaged by fire and during the restorations was altered in the Baroque style. The brick façade is simple and bare: it is a fine doorway and a round window with the symbols of the *Evangelists* at the sides. The bell tower was built in 1765. The magnificent interior is in the shape of an Egyptian cross: it has a single nave with double-lighted stained glass windows, trussed ceiling and a square apse with a four-lighted stained glass window. On the entrance wall are the remains of Salimbeni family tombs (13th-14th century). On the right wall of the nave, after the door to the cloister, is the 13th century *tomb of the Tolomei family*. In the right transept there is a *statue of St. Francis* by a pupil of Pisano's school. In the second chapel on the right of the tribune is the *tomb of Cristoforo Felici* by Urbano da Cortona (1462); the panel painting of the *Madonna and Child* on the altar of the first chapel is by Andrea Vanni. The glass window of the Tribune portrays *Pope Innocent III approving the Rule of St. Francis*, a modern work by Franz Xaver Zattler of Munich (1841-1916). The *Crucifixion* (1331) by Pietro Lorenzetti is in the left transept; *St. Louis of Anjou before Pope Boniface VII* and the *Martyrdom of Six Franciscan Friars at Ceuta* by Ambrogio Lorenzetti, are in the third chapel.

Above, left: *the basilica of San Francesco with the old door*, in a nineteenth century photo; opposite: *the big cloister*; below, from the left: *two views of the outside of San Francesco.*

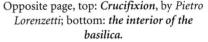

Opposite page, top: *Crucifixion*, by *Pietro Lorenzetti*; bottom: *the interior of the basilica.*

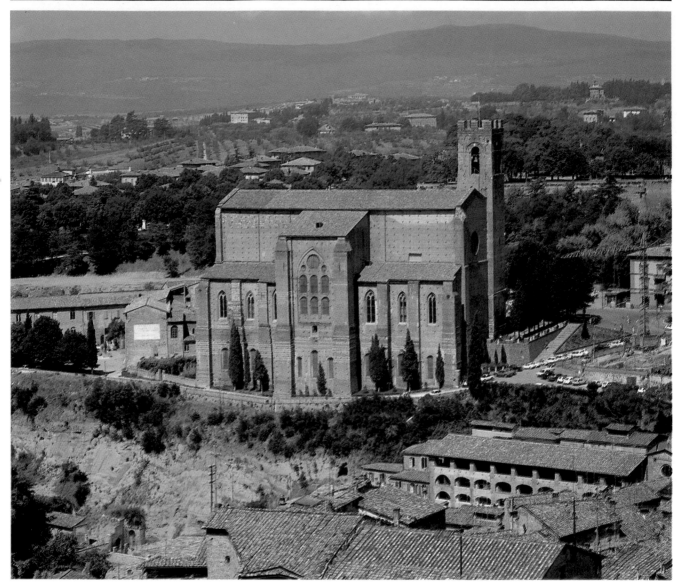

Aerial view of the Basilica of San Domenico;
below: *Saint Catherine* (detail) by *Andrea Vanni.*

SAN DOMENICO

The Dominicans began building this church in 1225 drawing inspiration from the monastic buildings of the Cistercian order. The fine bell tower was erected in 1340, and was originally higher than it is now, with a cusp. The battlements date from the 18th century. The chapels in the transept were built in the 14th century as was the grandiose ogival arch that joins the nave with the presbytery. The church was completed in 1465. The interior, in the shape of an Egyptian cross has a single nave and a trussed roof. Immediately on the right is the **Vault Chapel**, consisting of two great arches on pillars with a cross-vault (hence the name), and another pillar against which St. Catherine used to lean, according to tradition. On the altar is what is considered to be the most lifelike *portrait of St. Catherine* by Andrea Vanni. The artist knew the future patron saint of Italy personally, and he was her disciple. On the right of the nave is the **Chapel of St. Catherine,** built in 1488. The altar dedicated to the Blessed Ambrogio Sansedoni is at the end of the right transept. In the first chapel there is a *Virgin and Child* by Paolo di Giovanni Fei on the altar; on the right wall a *Madonna and Child with Saints, flanked by St. John the Baptist and St. Jerome,* by Matteo di Giovanni. On the High Altar there is a fine marble *ciborium* exquisitely sculpted by Benedetto da Maiano who also made the wonderful *candle-bearing angels* at the sides (1475). In the first chapel in the left transept there is a *Madonna and Child* by Sano di Pietro.

Nativity of the Virgin by *A. Casolani;* below: *the interior of the Basilica of San Domenico.*

CHAPEL OF ST. CATHERINE

This is the most important chapel in San Domenico. In the arch of the entrance are *Saint Luke* and *Saint Jerome* by Giovanni Antonio Bazzi, known as Sodoma, below are works by Francesco di Vanni, the *Blessed Raimondo da Capua*, the saint's confessor and biographer, and the *Blessed Tommaso Nacci Caffarini* who was her secretary. There is a fine 16th century graffito marble floor. The Head of St. Catherine is visible in the Neo-gothic (1931) reliquary-temple on the opposite wall (the body is in Santa Maria Sopra Minerva in Rome). The tabernacle is by Giovanni di Stefano (1466). Most of the frescoes in the chapel are by Sodoma: on the left side of the altar is the *Mystic Swoon of St. Catherine* and on the other, the *Ecstasy of the Saint*, two masterpieces that reveal the artist's consummate skill. On the left wall, again by Sodoma is the *Torture of Niccolò di Tuldo*, and on the right wall, the *Saint Frees a Possessed Woman* by Francesco di Vanni.

Above, left: *The mystic swoon of St. Catherine* by *Sodoma*; above, right: *Epiphany* (detail) by *Matteo di Giovanni*; opposite: *Tabernacle of St. Catherine* by *Giovanni di Stefano*.

The Portico of the Comunes of Italy.

THE HOUSE OF ST. CATHERINE

St. Catherine was born here on March 25, 1347. Nicolò Tommaseo described her as the "greatest woman in Christendom". The daughter of the dyer Jacopo Benincasa and Lapa di Nuccio Piagenti, Catherine was attracted to the religious life from childhood and opposed her parents' plans for her marriage. In 1363 she entered the Third Order of Dominicans, known as the Sisters of Penitence and led an intensely ascetic life. Her activities, however, were not only spiritual, but also social. She helped the poor, the sick and those condemned to death; she acted with heroic charity during the plague of 1374; and exerted herself to pacify rival cities. She was an ardent supporter of the Crusades, and of the Pope's return to Rome from his captivity in Avignon. She died in Rome on April 29, 1380 at the age of 30. Her letters give her a place among the greatest Italian women writers of all time. She was canonized by the Sienese Pope Pius II in 1461 and on June 18, 1939 was proclaimed Patron Saint of Italy by Pius XII. Sienese veneration for the saint caused her house to be transformed into a Sanctuary with a few modifications to the original structure. The **lower oratory** corresponds to the rooms of her father's dyeworks. The **upper oratory** comprises the former kitchen. The **church of the Holy Crucifix** was erected over the garden during the first half of the 17th century. The **bedroom oratory** was the saint's bedroom. The upper oratory has a fine coffered ceiling with gilt rosettes and a magnificent majolica floor. On the altar (the smoke stains from the hearth are still visible on the wall below) there is a panel painting by B. Fungai, portraying *St. Catherine Receiving the Stigmata*. A portico from the upper oratory leads the Church of the Crucifix attributed to Baldassarre Peruzzi. The name comes from the crucifix from which the Saint received the stigmata. In the right arm of the transept, on the altar, is the *Apotheosis of the Saint* by Rutilio Manetti; on the altar opposite is *St. Catherine before Gregory XI*, by Sebastiano Conca. The walls in the bedroom oratory are frescoed by Alessandro Franchi (1896) with *Seven Episodes from the Life of the Saint*, and on the altar there is Girolamo di Benvenuto's *The Saint Receives the Stigmata*. Next door is the cell where St. Catherine rested. The stone she used as a pillow can be see through a grating; the lantern for the night is in an urn along with the phial of aromas used for the sick, and what remains of the stick she used when she went to France.

PALAZZO CHIGI-SARACINI

(Via di Città) This palace, built between the 13th and 14th century was enlarged in 1787 and completely restored by Arturo Viligiardi between 1914 and 1922. The striking curved façade is made of stone up to the first story, the rest is brick with two rows of three-lighted windows with coats of arms above them. On the left there is a massive stone tower. As a whole, this magnificent palace is austere, but the effect is softened by the mingled colors of the brick and stone. The palace is the seat of the **Chigiana Music Academy** founded by Count Guido Chigi-Saracini in 1930. The atrium leads into the luminous **courtyard** that has a *well* in the middle and a frescoed portico on one side.

Palazzo Chigi-Saracini; right: *St. Jerome* (detail) by *Francesco di Vanni*; below: *Palazzo Piccolomini.*

PALAZZO PICCOLOMINI

(Via Banchi di Sotto) This Renaissance masterpiece was built to designs by Bernardo Rossellino in 1469. The elegant, two story building has a stone façade with double-lighted windows, topped by a fine cornice. It resembles the Palazzo Rucellai in Florence and Palazzo Piccolomini in Pienza. It houses the **State Archives** founded by Grand Duke Leopold II of Lorraine in 1858. The archives contain many documents concerning every aspect of city life. There are about sixty thousand parchments dating from the 8th century on, including the famous painted Tablets, covers of the tax registers for the *Biccherna* and *Gabella* used for the city-state's six-month account ledgers. The tablets were painted with coats of arms, religious and civic figures and portraits from 1258 on. The most important artists who worked on them included Ambrogio Lorenzetti, Giovanni di Paolo, Sano di Pietro, Cecco di Giorgio, Guidoccio Cozzarelli and Domenico Beccafumi.

VIA BANCHI DI SOPRA

This busy, typical Sienese street starts from the Merchants' Loggia which, in the old days was the seat of the tribunal appointed to resolve questions and disputes between merchants. This building, a typical example of the fusion of Gothic and Renaissance architecture, was built by Pietro del Minella between 1417 and 1428 to plans by San di Matteo. The palaces flanking the street include the Gothic **Palazzo Tolomei**, made entirely of stone, resembling a fortress in the lower part. The façade has two stories with elegant double-lighted windows, and it is believed to be the oldest private mansion in Siena since construction dates back to 1205. There is also the Gothic **Palazzo Cinughi** and **Palazzo Bichi-Ruspoli** built in 1250.

Palazzo Tolomei; bottom, left: *Madonna della Misericordia,* (detail) by *Benvenuto di Giovanni* (Monte dei Paschi collection); below: *Piazza Salimbeni with the monument to Sallustio Bandini* by *Tito Sarocchi* (1882).

PIAZZA SALIMBENI

The *monument to the economist Sallustio Bandini* by the Sienese sculptor, Tito Sarrocchi (1882) stands at the end of Via Banchi di Sopra. On the right is the Renaissance **Palazzo Spannocchi**, begun by Giuliano da Maiano for Ambrogio Spannocchi, treasurer to Pope Pius II, in 1473. The building, which has been restored has an elegant, smoothly rusticated façade with rectangular windows on the ground floor and two rows of double-lighted windows above. On the left is **Palazzo Tantucci** (1548) by Bartolomeo Neroni of Siena. At the end of the piazza stands the 14th century **Palazzo Salimbeni** which is built entirely of stone and was restored by Partini in 1879. The fine, three story façade is striking for the austerity of the lower walls, the elegant three-lighted windows on the first floor and the characteristic crenellated cornice.

SAN GIMIGNANO

A small town about 19 miles from Siena, San Gimignano is one of the most picturesque in Tuscany with its Medieval aspect, offset by many high towers and the original walls. It was important in the 12th and 13th centuries when it was a free city often at war with neighboring Volterra and torn by internal strife. In 1534 it came under the dominion of Florence. A typical product of its flourishing countryside is *Vernaccia* an excellent white wine, one of the best in Tuscany. One enters the 13th century walls from the spacious **Piazza Martiri di Monte Maggio**, passing through the **Gate of San Giovanni**. A street of the same name, flanked by old palaces goes up to the center of the town. Passing under the **Becci arch**, one enters the large,

triangular **Piazza della Cisterna** named after a 13th-14th century cistern there. It is surrounded by old buildings that include **Palazzo Tortoli** and the two **Ardinghelli towers**. Continuing, one comes to **Piazza del Duomo**. On the right there is the 13th-14th century **Palazzo del Podestà** with a loggia and high tower called **La Rognosa** ("Mangy"). Next to it stands the 13th century **Chigi Tower** and opposite the two **Salvucci Towers**. The **Collegiata** (cathedral) is on the left at the top of a long flight of steps. It is a Romanesque building that was rebuilt by Giuliano da Maiano in the 15th century. The interior, with three naves, contains many works of art. The interior of the façade and the beginning of the central nave are frescoed with the *Last Judgement, Hell*

Detail of the San Gimignano altarpiece with the Saint enthroned blessing the city by *Taddeo di Bartolo* (Museo Civico); below: *a panorama of San Gimignano.*

Piazza della Cisterna; above, right: t*he façade of the Collegiata cathedral;* opposite: *Palazzo del Podestà and the "Rognosa" tower;* below: *the Martyrdom of St. Sebastian* (detail) by *Benozzo Gozzoli.*

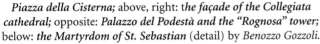

and *Paradise* by Taddeo di Bartolo (1393). Below this is the *Martyrdom of St. Sebastian* by Benozzo Gozzoli. The walls of the left and right aisles are covered with two fine fresco cycles depicting *Episodes from the Old and New Testaments* by Barna da Siena and Bartolo di Fredi (c. 1350). At the end, on the right, is the splendid **chapel of St. Fina**, a masterpiece by Benedetto and Giuliano da Maiano (1468), frescoed by Ghirlandaio with *Scenes from the Life of the Saint.* Ghirlandaio also painted the *Annunciation* in the outside loggia on the left side of the church. On the south side of Piazza del Duomo there stands the **Palazzo del Popolo** (late 13th century) which is the seat of the **Civic Museum** (*Majesty* by Lippo Memmi) and of the **Art Gallery** which can be reached by going up to the upper floors of the charming internal

Top, left: *Chapel of St. Fina*, by *Giuliano and Benedetto da Maiano*; right: *the Gate of San Giovanni*; bottom, left: *Palazzo Paltoni-Salvucci with the twin towers*; bottom, right: *the well outside the Gate of San Giovanni*.

courtyard. This gallery contains interesting works from the Florentine and Sienese schools. There is a *Crucifix* by Coppo di Marcovaldo, as well as two tondos by Filippino Lippi, paintings by Benozzo Gozzoli, Bartolo di Fredi and Mainardi. From the piazza one continues along the picturesque **Via S. Matteo** (with the **Pesciolini tower house**, late 13th century), then on to **Via Cellolese** to **Sant'Agostino**, a large Romanesque-Gothic church (late 13th century) that contains an *altar* by Benedetto da Maiano and outstanding frescoes by Benozzo Gozzoli (in the apse) depicting *Episodes in the Life of St. Augustine*. The town is dominated by the **Rocca** or castle from which there is truly a superb view.

INDEX